mardi gras beads

LOUISIANA TRUE books tell the stories of the state's iconic places, traditions, foods, and objects. Each book centers on one element of Louisiana's culture, unpacking the myths, misconceptions, and historical realities behind everything that makes our state unique, from above-ground cemeteries to zydeco.

mardi gras beads

DOUG MacCASH

Louisiana State University Press

Baton Rouge

Published by Louisiana State University Press
lsupress.org

LSU Press Paperback Original
Manufactured in the United States of America
First printing

Designer: Barbara Neely Bourgoyne
Typeface: Source Sans Variable
Printer and binder: Integrated Books International (IBI)

Library of Congress Cataloging-in-Publication Data
Names: MacCash, Doug, author.
Title: Mardi Gras beads / Doug MacCash.
Description: Baton Rouge : Louisiana State University Press, 2022.
Identifiers: LCCN 2021033540 (print) | LCCN 2021033541 (ebook) | ISBN 978-0-8071-7709-9
    (paperback) | ISBN 978-0-8071-7752-5 (pdf) | ISBN 978-0-8071-7751-8 (epub)
Subjects: LCSH: Carnival beads—Louisiana—New Orleans. | Carnival—Louisiana—New
    Orleans. | New Orleans (La.)—Social life and customs.
Classification: LCC GT4211.N4 M24 2022 (print) | LCC GT4211.N4 (ebook) |
    DDC 394.2509763/35—dc23
LC record available at https://lccn.loc.gov/2021033540
LC ebook record available at https://lccn.loc.gov/2021033541

For Melanie, Lucille, and Fisher, with all my love

contents

mardi gras beads

Introduction

Why anybody would read a book about Mardi Gras beads is a head scratcher. What could be more frivolous, right? Sensible people ought to be turning the pages of books about social history, geopolitics, and cultural identity; stuff like that. Well, here's the thing. Mardi Gras beads *are* a touchstone of social history, geopolitics, cultural identity, and stuff like that. Especially for those of us who live in the region where the big river begins the home stretch to the Gulf. Let's face it, Mardi Gras beads are us. They are our signature, our fingerprint, our smile. They're among the things that distinguish us. Mardi Gras beads are the twisted strands of DNA deep in the marrow of our bones. Close your eyes and visualize the Crescent City, and there's a good chance that strands of glistening, colorful, plastic pearls come to mind. They are a shorthand symbol seen in every airline poster and every beer ad that seeks to define us. In terms of New Orleans icons, they're right up there with a jazz musician blowing a horn beneath a streetlamp, a paddle wheeler plying the riverfront, and the three spires of St. Louis Cathedral stabbing toward heaven above a weather-tarnished statue of historically tarnished Andrew Jackson doffing his hat on the back of a rearing horse. Mardi Gras beads might be the hoariest of our hoary, self-distinguishing symbols.

Mardi Gras beads are like the Hawaiian leis of the southernmost metropolis on the Mississippi River. They are unmistakable markers of generosity and welcome, from the citizens of one of the most welcoming cities in the world to visitors and their fellow residents alike. They swing from the rearview mirrors of innumerable cars scattered across the country, indicating that the cars' owners are among the Carnival cognoscenti that have made the pilgrimage to America's greatest boozy blowout. Strands of airborne beads are the thing that makes New Orleans–style parades different from parades almost everywhere else. Here, parades aren't just spectacles. They're barely organized sporting events, with float riders pitching uncountable quantities of plastic necklaces to crowds of random catchers lining the curbs of city streets. The brilliant archaeologist and Carnival devotee Laurie A. Wilkie, who will be mentioned repeatedly in this book, calls the rider/spectator interaction the "throwing game."

Over the past hundred-plus years, float riders have thrown everything from elegant glass Art Deco–style chokers to surrealistically exaggerated necklaces with plastic beads as big as grapefruits. In New Orleans, a craving for beads is learned in infanthood, as is the skill of catching them. Kids are precariously strapped into seats atop teetering wooden ladders along the parade route and encouraged to raise their pudgy little arms and cry, "Throw me something, mister," as a rite of passage, just like being taught to ride a bike. Crescent City tykes are like ducks in a shooting gallery. They soon learn to snag flying plastic projectiles or be plastered by them in a ritual that would be deemed unconscionably dangerous and certainly outlawed in most of the civilized world. Children from other places would weep with despair if they knew what they're missing. The lust for plastic pearls persists into adulthood for an array of reasons. Over the past half-century, Mardi Gras beads have become entwined in a notorious custom in which Carnival celebrants use them as barter to entice others to disrobe. Tossing aside societal norms, thrill-seeking women gleefully reveal their upper regions and men expose their lower quadrants in exchange for strands of plastic orbs. It's a socioeconomic custom that has been intensely studied by scholars, including a respected university professor employed by the very same institution that published this book.

Speaking of socioeconomics, Mardi Gras beads don't come from within five thousand miles of New Orleans and never have, but they are revered here like nowhere else. Thus, they are a big business. Back in 1966, a *New Orleans Times-Picayune* culture columnist named Charles L. "Pie" Dufour wrote that parade-riders would spend $250,000 on beads and baubles to toss to the clamoring masses. According to New Orleans's reigning heavyweight champion bead importer, Dan Kelly, in 2020 riders spent $30 million to $40 million, maybe even more, to happily pelt Carnival crowds with imported plastic. One hundred and thirty shipping containers, each filled with 40,000 pounds of Chinese-made beads and other baubles, arrived at Kelly's warehouse in time for Carnival season 2020. That's 2,600 tons of tossable plastic. Kelly's competitors received at least that many container loads before the big day that year. All told, he suspects that the City That Care Forgot imported fifty million cheap, gaudy necklaces in 2020. As unlikely as it sounds, every strand is heavy with geopolitical history.

Mardi Gras beads were peripherally involved in one of Adolf Hitler's earliest European land grabs, they seem to have been used as barter by American servicemen fighting in the South Pacific in World War II, they may have been strung together by political prisoners in an Iron Curtain–era Czechoslovakian penal institution, and they are currently made by piece workers practicing a version of old-school capitalism in the United States' Communist frenemy the People's Republic of China. Archaeologists in the distant future will excavate the site of the legendary lost city of New Orleans and discover a sparkling strata of sediment embedded with zillions of mysterious polymer and glass orbs, plus beer cans and petrified fried-chicken bones. Those future underwater explorers (the whole place will be submerged by then, of course) will muse endlessly on the meaning of the enigmatic necklaces and the strange society they represented. Despite their obvious cultural importance, we, the current members of the Mardi Gras bead cult, don't give them much thought. Yet they are as tangled in the Crescent City gestalt as they become tangled in the branches of azalea trees along St. Charles Avenue. The glittering backstory of beads is what this book is all about.

1

It's Carnival Time

Carnival is an eons-old Catholic custom, conceived as a last hurrah before Lent, the season of contemplative self-deprivation leading to Easter. It supposedly ties in with pagan celebrations that reach back to Roman times and beyond. The last day of Carnival is Shrove Tuesday, aka Fat Tuesday, aka Mardi Gras. Explorer Pierre Le Moyne d'Iberville discovered the main channel of the Mississippi River on the last day of Carnival in 1699. To mark the occasion, he named the mudflat where he and his fellow sailors had come ashore Pointe du Mardi Gras. It's unknown whether Iberville and his men passed around a cask of burgundy in celebration. Probably not, considering his log entry, which doesn't sound terribly festive. "I had two cannister shots fired to give notice to the Indians, if there were some in the vicinity," he wrote. "There is no indication that any came. I climbed to the top of a nut tree as big as my body, but saw nothing other than canes and bushes." There's still not much to see at the site, besides tall grass, shrubs, and the ever-diminishing juncture of a continent of freshwater runoff and an ocean of intruding salt water.

In the 1930s beads were still scarce by today's standards,
but they had nonetheless become a Carnival icon. This is
a Rex parade float from 1935. Charles L. Franck Studio
Collection. © The Historic New Orleans Collection, acc.
no 1979.325.3729.

Fast-forward a century or so. New Orleans was a major metropolis in the early 1800s, the third largest city in the United States. Buoyed by river commerce, the cotton trade, sugar, and the despicable business of buying and selling humans, the city was as fat and rich as the crabs in Lake Pontchartrain, despite the nationwide economic depression that stifled profits at the time. There were no lavish float parades back then, but there were massive rambles of maskers on Mardi Gras morning, probably not much different from the foot parades, such as the Society of Saint Anne, that course through the narrow streets of the Bywater, Marigny, and French Quarter in the twenty-first century. A reporter with the *Picayune* newspaper, which had been putting ink on pulp for a mere two years at that point, tells us that the 1839 parade through the Vieux Carré—as the French Quarter is sometimes known—was particularly spectacular.

The parade was "longer, broader, further through and larger round than any procession that has preceded it in this good city," the reporter wrote. "Every window, balcony, stoop and doorway in Royal Street was filled." The chronicler described marchers costumed as "heathen and Christians, Turks and kangaroos, ancient Greeks and modern Choctaws, friars and beggars; knights and princesses, hard-favored ones at that; polar bears and chicken cocks." The long-dead writer's term "hard-favored" apparently means rugged-looking, or something like that. So it may have been a coy way of pointing out that some of the princesses were cross-dressing princes. The reporter also noted that more than one celebrant was outfitted as Old Corn Meal, an African American cornmeal vendor and entertainer who reportedly was the model for some minstrel performers. Another costumer impersonated Mrs. Trollope, a fearless British-born author whose 1832 book *Domestic Manners of the Americans* disdained slavery as well as other customs of the former colonists.

Mardi Gras authority Henri Schindler points out that, during this early Carnival era, the city earned the reputation as a place where "half the population takes turns watching and the other half parades." Schindler also believes that during that era, parade participants "tossed bonbons and flowers" to onlookers from carriages. Those small gestures of generosity may represent the earliest incarnation of the throwing game. The *Picayune* reporter doesn't mention the distribution of sweets or flowers in 1839, but does mention another custom that could also be a distant antecedent of the current bead cult. Among the assorted costumers, the writers tells us, "there was also a very 'floury' genius along, as some of our friends who got covered with meal can testify." The writer is referring to a flour bomber, an antebellum rapscallion who threw small sacks filled with powdered wheat that exploded into white clouds when they reached their unwary target. Battles between flour bombers reputedly caused the streets of the French Quarter to sometimes take on "the appearance of a snowstorm." And flour wasn't the only thing in the arsenals of Carnival miscreants. In 1852, a *Daily Picayune* reporter described crowd members who were "apparently determined to assert their right to scatter mud, flour and such missiles around them freely and promiscuously."

Flour bombing doesn't happen these days, maybe because it is explicitly forbidden in the city's Carnival code, which reads in part: "No Mardi Gras parade participant shall possess or have in his custody or control life-threatening objects or safety-threatening objects, including, but not limited to 'bomb bags.'" But flour-filled bags will forever have a place in Mardi Gras lore. They were among the first examples of pre-Lenten partiers engaging other pre-Lenten partiers by throwing stuff in their direction. Plus, flour bombing is one of the uncouth behaviors that gave the climax of Carnival a bad reputation among the more tight-jawed, chaos-adverse residents of mid-nineteenth-century New Orleans. In 1854, the *New Orleans Bee* newspaper reported that Mardi Gras had so declined that the celebration should be cut from the calendar entirely, in part because of wanton flour bombers. "Boys with bags of flour paraded the streets and painted Jezabels [*sic*] exhibited themselves in public carriages, and that is about all," the reporter dismissively wrote. "We are not sorry that this miserable annual exhibition is rapidly becoming extinct. It originated in a barbarous age and is worthy of only such."

Obviously, Carnival did not become extinct; it adapted. With its highly decorated, torch-lit, mule-draw floats, marching bands, pretentious theme (Milton's *Paradise Lost*), and pretend monarch, the Mistick Krewe of Comus parade in 1857 was a sensation. It was seen by some as a well-organized antidote to the existing undisciplined Mardi Gras celebrations that preceded it. The Comus parade was produced by former residents of Mobile, Alabama, and was inspired by an annual procession in that coastal city 144 miles to the east. The lavish parade was a gift to the citizenry. It was also the public expression of a secretive society for well-heeled white men. The Mobilians were part of an influx of new New Orleanians who established the exquisite neighborhoods above Canal Street. They were deemed "Americans."

The earlier inhabitants, who tended to live below Canal Street, were often called "Creoles."

The American parade template that the transplanted Mobilians established emphasized the distinction between those who rode atop the floats and those who stood in the muddy streets beneath them. That division between krewe members and all others was tailor-made for the future distribution of beads and other faux bounty, from the haves to the have-nots. Comus became the prototype for the parade of parades that followed. The short-lived Twelfth Night Revelers parade popped up in 1870, followed by Rex and Momus in 1872 and Proteus in 1882, all more or less in the Comus mold. Since Comus first rolled four years before the outbreak of the Civil War, it's likely it was originally lit by torchbearers—flambeaux, in New Orleans speak—who were enslaved men. Fourteen decades later, institutional racism would bring the hidebound krewe's parade to a halt. In 1992 Comus ceased rolling rather than abide by a proposed city ordinance that demanded integration. At this writing, some of the krewe's floats may still be moldering in its den.

Many Mardi Gras historians trace the Crescent City's current insatiable craving for trinkets and toys tossed from passing float parades to January 6, 1871. It was twelve days after Christmas, the Feast of Epiphany in the Catholic church, the day that, tradition tells us, the three wise men arrived at the humble nursery of the baby Jesus. Twelfth Night, as the evening is also known, is the traditional start of New Orleans's Carnival season, when residents drag their desiccated Christmas trees to the curb and begin gobbling king cake—a ring-shaped, sugar-coated pastry—at every opportunity. According to an account in the *Times-Picayune,* the second annual Twelfth Night Revelers parade that took place that evening included a caravan of painted, muslin-covered floats, illuminated by flickering flambeaux and accompanied by a marching band. As the parade approached, crowds along Canal, Camp, St. Charles, Carondelet, and Poydras streets cried, "Here they come, here they come."

The Revelers' theme that year was Mother Goose's nursery rhymes. But it wasn't Humpty Dumpty driving Mrs. Goose in a "grotesque" wagon made of brooms, or the "lovely" Red Riding Hood, or the "much abused" Cinderella that would make the parade so momentous in Mardi Gras history. The grand finale of the parade was jolly old St. Nick borne in a horse-drawn carriage with a gift basket on his back, dispensing stocking stuffers to the crowd as he shilled for a Canal Street general store known for its spectacular toy selection. "Very liberally did he along the route of procession distribute his presents," the *Times-Picayune* reporter wrote, "alternately out of a panier [basket/backpack] with which his back was encumbered, and out of a box marked 'From Piffet's, Canal Street,' standing at his feet." It was a game-changing moment. Like sharks tasting blood, New Orleans parade-goers had become acquainted with anonymously, democratically tossed parade treasure for the first time, and they collectively hungered for more. Would they ever be satisfied with the mere aesthetic pleasure of a passing series of lavishly decorated floats again? Would the gift of an occasional bonbon or flower ever suffice again? Would the cries of "Here they come" eventually be replaced with "Throw me something, mister"? The answers are: Nope, nope, and you betcha.

It was just a year after the ersatz Santa pioneered the institutional tossing of gifts from a Carnival parade that a handful of young, civic-minded Crescent City associates conceived a Mardi Gras morning spectacle that would introduce a newly minted mythical character, Rex, the King of Carnival. The King—a successful businessman or admired professional in disguise—would proclaim the close of stores, offices, and schools on Mardi Gras day and bid the populous to dress up, dance, and debauch. From the start, Rex was a publicity ploy, meant to attract crowds to New Orleans during the economic doldrums following the Civil War. Dr. Stephen Hales is the affable, astute historian of the Rex parading organization. In his book *Rex: An Illustrated History of the School of Design,* Hales explained the strategy like so: "Proclamations inviting all to join the Mardi Gras celebrations appeared in the form of posters and brochures distributed up and down the railway lines and in steamship terminals connecting New Orleans to the rest of the country. Visitors enthusiastically accepted the invitation, and the New Orleans Carnival became a favorite tourist destination."

The first Rex was a thirty-three-year-old mustachioed banker named Lewis Salomon, who raised the five grand necessary to pay for the first parade. The former Confederate soldier wore a borrowed velvet and ermine robe from a local playhouse's production of *Richard III* and rode a bucking horse that slobbered on his costume. On the fiftieth anniversary of the first Rex parade, Salomon told a *Times-Picayune* reporter that "more than 60,000 persons jammed onto the neutral ground of Canal Street for that first arrival of Rex. Quite a crowd for those days and even now."

"Little has been written about Salomon other than that he was Jewish," wrote Carnival authority Errol Laborde in a 2015 online essay, adding that the first Rex's background has been "treated with a certain irony given Carnival's Christian origins." But by the time of the inaugural Rex parade, Salomon had converted to Catholicism. "He would spend most of his adult life as a devout and philanthropic Catholic," Laborde wrote, "though his burial site would be a Jewish cemetery in Brooklyn." Salomon's crowning as King of Carnival was, in a way, a historical confluence. Lewis Salomon's great-great-grandfather Haym had helped fund George Washington's army in order to cast off a gaudy monarchy. Less than a century later, Lewis had funded the founding of a new gaudy monarchy—albeit a pretend one. In the twenty-first century, Rex is known both for its Mardi Gras morning parade and its annual donation of $1 million to New Orleans schools. It's an intriguing coincidence that the first Rex parade took to the streets just one year after Santa's ride. And it's irresistible to imagine that the jolly old elf had inspired participants in the inaugural Rex parade to toss gifts to the tens of thousands of onlookers. The thing that deflates such speculation is that none of the newspaper recollections of the first Rex parade include mention of beads, or throws of any kind for that matter.

It's impossible to say when the first costumed rider climbed aboard a float clutching a silk bag stuffed with slender strands of glass beads and other trinkets to be tossed to members of the parade audience. Way back on January 14, 1834, an advertisement appeared in the columns of *The Bee* newspaper, announcing the arrival of 11 boxes of glass beads from Venice, which had gone on sale January 3 at a Royal Street store. Since the beads were imported on the cusp of the Carnival season, it's tantalizing to imagine they were meant to become parade favors, but there's no proof whatever.

"There was probably never a time that there wasn't a personal exchange of this or that," Dr. Hales speculated. "It was an ad hoc thing, with no sort of organization. What you would have had was a rider with six bracelets waiting to throw to six people he knew on the route." Searching through history for clues to the origins of the throwing custom is like "following breadcrumbs scattered in the forest. You find an article here, a remembrance there," he said. But, like poor Hansel and Gretel, you're still liable to end up lost in the woods.

The first Rex parade was made up entirely of marchers and horsemen, but in no time the procession included highly decorated floats à la Comus. By the time the Rex parade was a quarter-century old, at least some of the riders on those floats threw small gifts to dignitaries, if not necessarily to the ordinary folk in the crowd. In a March 3, 1897, article, a *Daily Picayune* reporter described the scene as the Rex parade reached Mayor Walter "Chew" Flower's Gallier Hall review stand, where a delegation of visitors from a Chicago political organization honored the King of Carnival with their umbrellas, raised in a military-style salute. "There were greetings to individual members from different cars as the procession moved by," the journalist wrote. "Souvenirs were thrown to them from the cars and the advertising vans on the streets."

Mayor Flower had a sinister past. The former *Picayune* reporter-turned-politician was elected with the knowledge that he was a member of the 1891 mob that murdered eleven Italians held in the city jail, an event so stunning that it strained diplomatic relations between Italy and the United States. The captives had been accused, and most had been acquitted, of murdering the chief of police. In his book *Vendetta: The True Story of the Largest Lynching in U.S. History,* Richard Gambino postulates that, "With Flower's election, the city of New Orleans completed its overwhelming endorsement of lynching as a way of controlling ethnic minorities." Flower's participation in the savage spree, which included shootings and public hangings, had apparently only polished his popularity among his peers because, in 1898, the Rex riders rained throws on him. As a reporter noted in a February 23 *Times-Picayune* article, "while the show was passing the City Hall, Mayor Flower took his stand, central on the platform, and gave greeting to the occupants of each float. From each van he was showered with trinkets of one character or another and was obliged to catch the most of them in his silk hat."

"Trinkets of one character or another" is the most specific description available in newspaper archives until finally, on February 18, 1912, a story appeared in the *New Orleans Item* that includes what may be the first specific mention of beads. That Mardi Gras promised to attract "the largest crowd New Orleans has entertained in ten years," according to the unnamed author. The estimate, based on the intuition of railroad employees watching tourists disembarking from trains, was "as high a figure as 50,000." An article positioned lower on the page titled "What Mardi Gras Is" was a scene-setter, written days before Fat Tuesday 1912, in which the journalist described energetic male revelers peacocking before eligible young women seated on the balconies and bleachers along the parade route. "Through several miles of streets they go, greeting their friends on the way and passing, now and then, a stand before some club where a bevy of society girls watch eagerly for some familiar figure. On they go, scattering trinkets and beads through the crowds and dancing without stopping." Beads! Since the *Item* reporter was writing a pre–Mardi Gras story meant to tell readers what to expect, it's fair to assume that beads were a predictable part of Carnival consciousness before 1912. But that doesn't mean they were as important to the character of the parades as they would become. For the next decade, they would be mentioned sporadically in the press, but not consistently.

The Rex den is a nondescript warehouse along a busy avenue in New Orleans's Central City. Most of the structure is a depot for the krewe's fleet of floats, which are lavishly redecorated each year. The den is also appointed with a spacious dressing room for the four-hundred-plus members to don their disguises before the parade and a rudimentary store where custom-designed Rex beads and other throws are sold to members. There's also a sort of museum, where the fabulous gowns, faux jewelry, and antique accessories of past Rex royalty are displayed in glass cases. The aforementioned Dr. Hales is not merely the Rex organization's historian. In 2017, the Utah-born pediatrician, who had taken up residence in the Crescent City in 1975, was crowned Rex, the symbolic ruler for a day of his adoptive city. In the world of New Orleans Carnival custom, it was an immeasurable honor. That was Dr. Hales, wearing a snowy faux beard and golden crown, passing his scepter over his subjects as he proceeded along St. Charles Avenue on his canopied throne, atop the royal float. Rex is generally absolved from reflexively tossing throws to the bauble-hungry masses. But most float riders, Hales said, find themselves in "a cone of loud noise, beckoning, begging and cajoling" for beads and other coveted trinkets. Everywhere arms are stretched upward.

Which makes the 1913 photograph by Herbert J. Harvey, displayed in the Rex den, so remarkable. The panoramic black-and-white picture captures the Rex parade as it turns from St. Charles Avenue onto Canal Street. A mule-drawn float at the focal point of the photo is adorned with the sculpted torso of a mythological hero of some sort. A float rider can be seen standing stiffly on the bow. Trombonists follow in the street behind. Spectators enjoy what must have been spectacular bird's-eye views of the procession from windows and balconies above storefronts and restaurants. That Mardi Gras morning, a shoulder-to-shoulder throng of onlookers crowded Canal Street—which was said to be the widest street in the world, by proud New Orleanians anyway. Thousands of fedoras and bowlers, and various examples of women's winter headwear, bob above the multitude. A daredevil has climbed what may have been an early traffic light for a vista. That's what can be seen. "But," Hales asks during tours of the den, "what don't you see?" Another, more careful glance at the photo and it still may not register that there's a singular characteristic of contemporary Carnival parade crowds that is missing. What is it? "There's not a hand raised, not a bead," Hales points out finally. And he's right. The tiny black-and-white photographic figures seem content to watch the passing spectacle without clamoring for the tawdry treasure that would so agitate onlookers at future parades. We can be sure that beads were part of Carnival tradition by 1912, but the antique photo proves that, in 1913, as the young Louis Armstrong worked on his chops in New Orleans's so-called Colored Waifs Home for Boys and soon-to-be assassin Gavrilo Princip was somewhere in Sarajevo seething with the anti-Austrian anger that would precipitate World War I, beads and baubles weren't yet crucial to the Carnival experience.

2

The Arms Race

For only the sixth time in history, Carnival was officially canceled in 1918, as droves of New Orleans doughboys shipped off to France to help turn the tide on the Germans in World War I. As an *Item* newspaper writer gravely intoned in a January 27 story, wartime sacrifice had "resulted in the abandonment of the great, globe-famous Mardi Gras of New Orleans, and February 12 this year will be only Shrove Tuesday and not the great day of the year when Orleanians and thousands of visitors join in the homage to the patron idol of 'the city that care forgot.'"

A story in the *Daily States* newspaper applauded Mayor Martin Behrman's decision to ban masking on Mardi Gras day, citing both the inappropriateness of celebrating with "soldiers and sailors dying daily and the whole country on the basis of thrift and economy," and also security reasons. "We have in our midst many spies and enemy aliens," the writer explained. "Only unceasing vigilance on the part of the police, soldiery and agents of justice restrains them from sabotage and other crimes. To permit masking at this time would only be to invite them to commit these crimes." The warning wasn't as far-fetched as it may seem. On July 30, 1916, an enormous stockpile of explosives and ammunition stored on an island in New York harbor mysteriously detonated, sending shock waves across Lower Manhattan and spraying the Statue of Liberty with shrapnel. Though it wasn't known at the time, it was determined years later that the cataclysm had been the work of German saboteurs.

If war weren't enough, the rampaging Spanish flu was another cause for great consternation. Between September 8, 1918, and March 15, 1919, almost one in one hundred New Orleans citizens died from the virulent virus—more than three thousand in all—casting a pall over all else. If Mayor Behrman had not called off the Fat Tuesday 1918 fete, the mingling masses might very well have fanned the flames of the contagion—as happened a little more than a century later when the coronavirus gained a foothold in New Orleans during the climax of Carnival 2020.

When the so-called War to End All Wars ended on November 11, 1918, the populace poured onto the street in swarms in what a *Times-Picayune* story described as "a celebration such as New Orleans, although noted for such things, has never seen before." Charles Janvier, a former King of Carnival and spokesman for the Rex organization, argued for the continuation of Carnival as soon as possible and vowed to provide a parade whenever the city government permitted, as soon as March 4, 1919. Janvier called for "celebrating the war's end by a Carnival that would outrival anything Venice or Nice ever attempted." But big celebratory processions weren't deemed appropriate. After all, American servicemen and servicewomen had yet to return from

In 1952, the United States had entered a nuclear standoff, but it wasn't the only arms race taking place. The quest for beads caused competition among krewes, who sought to please their crowds. This photo of a Krewe of Carrollton float is dated circa 1952. Photo by Homer Emory Turner, Gift of Ms. Beverly T. Lynds. Courtesy of The Historic New Orleans Collection, acc. no. 2002.84.18.

Europe. For reasons difficult to discern, some civic leaders debated whether Mardi Gras should be reinstated at all, ever. According to newspaper accounts from the time, a cabal of businessmen hoped to replace Mardi Gras with a 200- to 250-mile automobile race, like the one that had taken place in Indianapolis since 1911. The proposed race would circulate on a minimally banked track from downtown to Lake Pontchartrain and back. But New Orleans resisted such a radical cultural change.

In the end, Carnival was not canceled in 1919, not entirely anyway. Two weeks before Mardi Gras, Mayor Behrman announced that, though the large parades, including Comus, Momus, Proteus, and Rex, would remain on the sidelines in the first year after war, individual maskers and smaller parading organizations such as the Mysterious Babies, the Jefferson City Buzzards, and the Easy Riders would be welcome to take to the streets. As a *Times-Picayune* reporter put it, if New Orleanians "feel the need for a celebration, they are at liberty to start one of their own." But, according to at least one onlooker, they just weren't feeling it. In the March 4 *Item,* a reporter described the last day before Lent as a "Pathetic Reminder of Old-Time Glories." In twisted Elizabethan prose, the reporter typed: "Came Tuesday another Mardi Gras Day, and with it just the wistful echo, the subdued suggestion of the unleashed revelry and brilliant magnificence of years past. . . . On the streets appeared, early in the morning, the young and those who refused to be dispirited, garbed in the fading splendor of costumes of other days. But they were only silhouettes of the past on the wall of time."

A reporter with the rival *Times-Picayune* wrote a story titled "Carnival Spirit Rampant, Despite Absence of Rex," which presented a more glass-half-full approach. "With the war so recently concluded, this was to have been a modest, even a somber Carnival," the reporter explained. But, "spontaneously, without plan or organization, hundreds upon hundreds of masked revelers thronged the city's streets. . . . Decorated wagons, automobiles and trucks, loaded with hand organs, string bands and even a calliope, and filled with merrymakers, were seen." So, it seems, the exuberance of Mardi Gras 1919 lay in the eye of the beholder. Perhaps it was a contemplative, restrained conclusion to Carnival. Perhaps it was a cathartic blowout. Either way, there doesn't seem to be any mention of beads or baubles of any sort being tossed around.

After war and pestilence came Prohibition. At the dawn of the Roaring Twenties, the Eighteenth Amendment went into effect, corking America's consumption of debilitating demon rum—at least America's legal consumption of debilitating demon rum. It probably goes without saying that the citizenry of the City that Care Forgot did not unanimously buy into the so-called Noble Experiment. In fact, according to a nationwide survey of social workers conducted in 1926, New Orleans was the "wettest" city in ostensibly "dry" America. Nonetheless, the criminalization of alcohol complicated matters as Carnival approached. How on earth were the Mardi Gras parades scheduled to resume in 1920 supposed to roll without proper lubrication? If the government's banning of booze weren't demoralizing enough, as Fat Tuesday 1920 dawned, northern winds off of Lake Pontchartrain blew in a bone-chilling New Orleans winter rain. Rex was the only large-scale parade to take to the streets despite the inclemency. A

1920 photo that appears in Henri Schindler's book *Mardi Gras: New Orleans* captures Rex atop his royal float waving to his subjects, many of whom watch from beneath black umbrellas. The outstretched arms of a few soggy members of the crowd and the gestures of some of Rex's entourage suggest the possibility that prizes were being tossed, though none can be seen.

Whether they awaited parade booty or just a glimpse of the king, Rex's subjects were certainly loyal, as a *Times-Picayune* reporter noted in a marvelous narrative in the Ash Wednesday newspaper. "A chill air smote their ribs, vagrant streams of water from o'erhanging sheds trickled down their necks . . . yet steadfastly they stood and waited for the parade that is never on time." A little chilly rib smiting wouldn't have fazed the guest of honor in the mayor's box at Gallier Hall that morning. General "Black Jack" Pershing, the square-jawed commander of the American Expeditionary Forces in France, had just helped defeat Kaiser Wilhelm's army in history's grimmest war to date. The King of Carnival added another decoration to the United States' highest-ranking soldier's collection, dubbing Pershing "the Duke of Victory," to the appreciative cheers of the crowd. It's unknown if the general was also pelted with trinkets by some masked float riders. Possibly so, though nobody mentioned it in print.

However, the *Times-Picayune* writer cited above encountered parade debris that assures us the custom of throwing toys and trinkets, probably including beads, had survived the hiatus from 1917 to 1920. "There was quite a litter in front of an uptown apartment house where the parade had paused—empty boxes, shreds of paper and broken favors," the reporter noted. The accumulation of detritus was conspicuous enough that a young girl reportedly asked her mother, "Can God see all this mess?" When told yes, the child declared, "Well, if I was God, I'd tell the janitor." There's a chance that among the "favors" that Rex's masked men had dispensed that year might have been, of all things, throat lozenges. As the *Times-Picayune* scribe observed, when Rex appeared, his subjects "croakingly greeted him, straining their voices into the semblance of a cheer. Then they ate another cough drop, truly the most appropriate favor distributed during the parade," though the reporter may have simply meant that lozenges were shared among shivering members of the crowd.

By 1921 the tossing of trinkets from the Rex parade by at least some of the masked riders had been part of Carnival for at least a quarter-century. But many Mardi Gras history authorities, Dr. Stephen Hales included, believe that in 1921 the practice reached a new plateau. They believe that, in preparation for the golden anniversary of the Rex parade that year, the King of Carnival, Sidney J. White, commanded all participants in the parade to toss trinkets to the crowd, thereby transforming the individual, voluntary dispensing of souvenirs into an enduring institution. According to Henri Schindler, other organizations followed suit. "The krewes of Momus and Proteus were soon tossing baubles into the night too and the practice became a fixture of Carnival," he wrote. Comus resisted the change longer than the other organizations, according to Schindler, but eventually succumbed. Dr. Hales said that you can either thank or blame Rex for the century-long "arms race" that followed, as parades vied to woo and reward their devotees with more and more airborne gifts. "Arms race" is the perfect, poetic pun, because it both describes the upward stretched forelimbs of the experienced bead catcher and the Cold War–era nuclear weapon rivalry between the United States and the Soviet Union that gave us phrases like "throw weight" and "mutually assured destruction." "Throw weight" originally meant warhead efficiency, but could easily be applied to the heft of Carnival baubles or float-rider generosity. Mutually assured destruction is how environmentalists view the glut of plastic generated by typical Carnival parades from the late twentieth century into the present.

If Rex decreed the birth of the throwing game in 1921, then let this book mark the centennial of that moment. The trouble with the theory is that no reference to the King of Carnival's 1921 edict appears to exist. For that matter, no specific reference to beads or any sort of throws being tossed during the 1921 Carnival popped up in the newspapers of the time. That doesn't make the story untrue, of course. The belief that tossing small gifts from floats became institutionalized in 1921 may be an instance of accurate oral tradition. The absence of proof aside, that year would have been the perfect moment for Rex to call on krewe members to make gift giving an official part of their parading habits. After a pair of Fat Tuesdays curtailed by the Keiser and another ruined by cold rain, Carnival 1921 was a long-awaited dawn. Hotel rooms filled. Passenger ships anchored at the wharves. The new Druids parade debuted, the weather was agreeable, and, as a *Times-Picayune* headline writer put it, "wild rollicking and happy crowds" celebrated Mardi Gras. What better time for the King of Carnival to decree the tossing of beads in honor of the reborn celebration?

That year, the Harcol Film Company produced a silent movie that was touted as "the first complete picturization of a New Orleans Mardi

Gras day." The motion picture, which was made with "the special authorization of the Rex organization," may have slipped away into cinema history without a trace. But another flickering film that reputedly captures the 1921 Rex procession still exists, and it's as close as our smartphones. Search YouTube for a fifty-three-second video titled "Mardi Gras 1921: Rare Early Twentieth Century New Orleans Footage!" The brief motion picture, which was produced by the Ford Motor Company's advertising department and is part of the collection of the National Archives and Records Administration, seems to capture trinket tossing. As the convoy of shimmering Carnival floats makes a left-hand turn, masked riders certainly seem to briskly underhand objects into the crowd. The softly focused film defies close analysis, yet it's hard to imagine what else the long-buried float riders might have been doing, if they were not softballing Mardi Gras throws.

Rex was not alone in institutionalizing gifts as part of the Carnival gestalt. At about the same time the King of Carnival's men were making beads an integral part of the big party, another parading organization was pioneering the first signature throw. Near the end of the first decade of the twentieth century, the Zulu Social Aid and Pleasure Club foot parade joined Rex as a highlight of Mardi Gras morning, and by 1915 the Zulus had incorporated floats into their procession. The Black parading group was initially inspired in 1909 by a vaudeville-era comedy called *There Never Was and Never Will Be a King Like Me,* centered on the Zulu people of South Africa. William Story, the first Zulu king, wore a crown made from a lard can and carried a staff made of a banana stalk. Instead of masks, the Zulus wore face makeup. "Half a hundred ferocious black and white painted warriors bearing spears" were expected to appear in the 1921 Zulu parade, according to a preview in the *Item.* In 1922 "the King of Zululand," Herbert Permillion, reportedly appeared "clad in the jungle grass, the armbands, the glittering crown, the anklebands and the brilliant breastplate of royalty . . . and nothing more." A year later, King Joseph Kahoe wore "the finest suit of tiger skin." As was customary at the time, the Zulu queens who accompanied the kings were male members of the club who had cross-dressed for the occasion. In 1924, King A. Hippolite's float was a wagon drawn by mules that "represented a coconut grove, with real palms and with much tinsel."

In keeping with the coconut-grove aesthetic, somewhere along the line, riders in the Zulu parade had begun lobbing coconuts to parade-goers. Though it's unclear exactly when the custom began, by 1928 Zulu coconuts made an appearance in the papers. That year, King H. C. Hicks "tossed an imperial cocoanut to [Mayor] Jimmy Walker," according to a story in the *Times-Picayune,* momentarily reaching across the racial chasm that divided New Orleans. A 1929 film in the University of South Carolina Libraries' archive captures King Zulu addressing the crowd from his float. "It's so great to have this opportunity to come from way in the Zulu part of the country to the great city of New Orleans, and so proud to see the congregation out as [big] as it is," the king intones. A rider in a subsequent float passes a coconut to a member of the crowd. Based on the almost five-minute film, we can conclude that Zulu hadn't yet incorporated bead tossing into its parading customs.

At the time, Zulu coconuts were probably nothing more than examples of the natural palm seeds. But in terms of the history of

Carnival throws, they were decades ahead of their time, because they were identifiable. The souvenirs dispensed at Comus, Rex, Momus, and Proteus were more or less the same; beads were beads, toys were toys. But coconuts were unmistakably the signature of the Zulu Social Aid and Pleasure Club. It wasn't until 1960, when Rex riders began tossing aluminum coins marked with the krewe crest, that another parade caught up with Zulu in the branding game. Since then, krewes have emblazoned their logos on everything from beads to plush toys to cups to footballs to Frisbees to the coins mentioned above, which are known as doubloons.

Zulu coconuts are no longer simply coconuts. Somewhere in the intervening years, riders began painting them gold and, more recently, elaborately decorating them with paint and glitter. In the twenty-first century many krewes have emulated Zulu, inventing signature decorated objects of their own, including women's shoes, purses, plastic crabs, plastic goblets, old-fashioned 45-rpm records, and so forth. Glittered and bejeweled objects are a ubiquitous and uniquely New Orleans art form that can be traced directly back to Zulu. In the 1920s, as Zulu pioneered club-centric gifts and Rex codified the tradition of tossing beads, sometimes unpredicted players popped up in the throwing game. According to a *Times-Picayune* account, as the 1924 Zulu parade passed the Silverstein's store on Rampart Street, the proprietor "threw out scores of souvenirs into the streets," causing a momentary "cataclysm" as paraders scrambled for the (undescribed) gifts. "It seemed for a few minutes that the parade was over," but order was soon restored.

It's impossible to say exactly what Mardi Gras beads looked like in the late nineteenth and early twentieth centuries. Then, as now, they were inexpensive, transitory trinkets that didn't become treasured family heirlooms or part of museum collections. They were probably glass, because most manufactured beads were glass. They were probably round, because they were sometimes described as "pearls." Most strands were probably short and slim by today's standards, because the arms race was still in its infancy. There weren't yet Mardi Gras bead suppliers per se, so riders bought their throws from ordinary stores. Nine days before Fat Tuesday 1922, a salient line of text jumps out at the top of the full-page Maison Blanche department store ad in the *New Orleans States* Sunday paper. There, above the sale-priced gas ranges, women's fine slippers, and dainty cottage aprons, the department store offered a dozen strings of fancy beads for 75 cents, or $11.45 in 2020 dollars. "Attention Float Maskers," the ad reads, "we've gathered a lot of fancy bead necklaces suitable for throwing at the 'Mardi Gras' crowds. Very pretty and extremely low in price."

Though the price may have been "extremely low," by the magic of Mardi Gras, the value of those beads psychologically soared as they flew from the white-gloved hands of float riders to the throng. "What a scramble was created with the passing of floats and wagons distributing things!" wrote a reporter in the February 28, 1922, *Item*. "As the Rex maskers tossed strings of pearls, watches and brooches and such like toys, the crowd, quiet before, burst into power like an [artillery] shell. Happy the man with a telegraph pole reach," the writer continued, "and happy the girl who looked in ox-eyed gratitude at her successful escort." Strings of pearls were to become a seasonal addiction among New Orleanians, but in 1922 it wasn't the only habit-forming item tossed willy-nilly to outstretched hands. "It didn't matter what was being distributed," the *Item* reporter continued with a hint of cynicism, "people couldn't get enough of it. Hundreds of boys followed the advertising wagons, some of which tossed out a largesse of cigarettes or gum, and some merely circulars. Immense crowds of boys followed each wagon, like a comet's trail."

Chances are, twenty-first-century readers would uniformly disapprove of the dispersal of cigarettes to youthful parade-goers. Some students of Carnival history disapprove of the advent of throws of any kind, for aesthetic reasons. Henri Schindler believes that, starting in the 1920s, the presence of flying beads and baubles ruined the sublime theatrical nature of early Carnival parades. As Schindler described them, the floats were awe-inspiring throwbacks to an earlier time, in which the riders practiced an antique sort of performance art in which they stood as still as marble statues amidst elaborate sets. "The architecture of the floats, like baroque palaces and altars, overwhelmed the viewer with wonder," he wrote. "To revel in their trappings was to abandon one's sense of self, time, or place, and to experience the transforming power of art. The introduction of trinkets broke this spell." The spell wasn't entirely broken. To this day, some Carnival parades are enthralling artistic spectacles produced by master designers, sculptors, and painters. And it is certainly possible to abandon oneself to their transforming power, though it's best to do so from a safe distance, beyond the reach of flying beads and other missiles.

From an artistic point of view, throws might have been a distraction from the visual purity of the earliest float parades, but there was no going back. By the flapper era, necklaces and other favors had become as much a part of Carnival as trick-or-treat candy is to Halloween.

On February 17, 1931, all was not well. The economic catastrophe known as the Great Depression had taken hold across the land, as stock-market investors lost fortunes, laborers lost jobs, and farmers lost their land. Flamboyant, left-leaning Louisiana governor Huey Long clamored for the rich to share their wealth with those less fortunate, doubtlessly sending shivers up the spines of residents of St. Charles Avenue, New Orleans's mansion row, where the major parades rolled. But it was Mardi Gras morning, and Mayor Arthur O'Keefe put the worries of the world behind and made his way to his viewing box at Gallier Hall to take in the pageant of the Rex parade. As was the custom, the costumed gentlemen aboard the rattling floats would toss tokens to the mayor and his entourage, faux jewelry that any sensible man would recognize as worthless. But to the soon-to-be-notorious kid who crouched in the street near the mayor's box, Rex trifles were treasure. The kid "shouted himself hoarse," a *Times-Picayune* reporter wrote, but "his efforts were futile." In desperation, the boy made a bold move. According to the reporter, when a float stopped near the mayor's perch, "the lad lunged forward and before anyone knew what had happened, he was on the float with both hands buried in a box. . . . The float moved forward and the boy leaped out into the crowd, bearing almost enough bracelets and necklaces to start a Mardi Gras parade of his own."

The young Dillinger's exact identity is lost to history. He may have been a harbinger of Depression-era lawlessness. Or, more likely, he was just an early exemplar of the reckless, bone-deep lust for beads that typifies Carnival in the consciousness of so many New Orleanians. What you notice while perusing newspaper clippings from the 1930s is that general terms such as "trinkets," or "novelties," or "gifts" have lost ground to specific references to beads. During the ensuing decades, float riders would toss everything from collectable doubloons to custom-made plastic drinking cups to edible Moon Pie cakes to Frisbee-style flying disks, bamboo spears, bikinis, internally lit rubber balls, coconuts, and an endless menagerie of plush stuffed animals. But beads would rule. It was in the 1930s that strands of glass pearls came to signify Carnival and thereby the Crescent City itself. A newsreel shot by cameraman Leroy Orr during the 1931 Rex and Zulu parades captures the bead-tossing custom of the time. Beads were certainly less common than they are in the twenty-first century, but they were plentiful. The masked riders of the Rex parade have stocked various sizes, from bracelets to yard-long strands, which they toss underhand to the crowds below them and overhand to more distant celebrants. The riders in the Zulu parade do not seem to throw beads. Instead, at least one rider dispenses small cards or pamphlets.

"Proteus promises to be generous with his beads provided you all keep back from the floats," cautioned a 1933 *Item* column by A. Labas. "If you don't get a bead from Rex or Comus on Mardi Gras Day it doesn't count," advised a 1934 story in the *Item*. Luckily, the same story reported that "Beads fell like rain" from the Rex procession. An enigmatic feel-good story in a 1935 issue of the *Item* reported that an empathetic teenage girl named Rita sent a strand of beads caught at the Rex parade to another teen named Alice in Fall River, Massachusetts, who was suffering from "an inverted stomach." Alice said she was "thrilled to get a string of beads from New Orleans' Mardi Gras." How Rita and far-away Alice became acquainted is unexplained. But what is clear is that the bead cult had already spread beyond the Crescent City limits.

A popular tune of the time titled "Way Down Yonder in New Orleans" described the city as a "land of dreamy scenes." But the abject racism and institutional inequity of the era was nightmarish. As Mardi Gras beads came to symbolize Carnival, they also served as props in situations that illustrate the segregationist ethos of the time. In a 1931 *Times-Picayune* story, "one of the negroes" who was carrying the banner bearing the title of the Punch-and-Judy float in the Rex parade laid down his sign in order to retrieve a strand of beads for himself. "But his exultation was short-lived," we're told, "as a policeman made him give them to a lady in the reviewing stand." Since her race remained unstated, we can assume the lady in the reviewing stand was white.

A slice-of-life story in the *States,* drawn from the same parade, provides a more nuanced peek at the Jim Crow gestalt. It centers on an elderly Black woman, whom the writer describes as "a typical Southern mammy" awaiting the Rex parade on St. Charles Avenue, hopeful that she will receive beads. The "beautifully gowned," presumably white, woman standing beside her, who waved her "jeweled hands" at the float riders, had similar hopes. But it was the elderly Black woman who won out when "a gloved hand reached out from a float toward the old negress." The float rider called out "Aunt Millie" and placed "a gorgeous string of beads" in the old woman's hands.

As the parade passed, the well-dressed white woman, who had apparently been denied beads by all of the men of Rex, offered to buy the beautiful string of beads from the old woman. But she was rebuffed. No, the old woman said, "them beads came from my white folks." The moral of the story seems to be that the well-heeled white woman might have expected preferential treatment under ordinary circumstances, but the blue-blooded Rex masker expressed exemplary values by shining his largesse on a beloved family servant instead. Or something to that effect.

Blue-blooded President Franklin Roosevelt paid a visit to New Orleans in April 1937, speeding along Canal Street in the back of a convertible in the spring air. Unfortunately, an *Item* columnist wryly noted, "the President didn't throw a single string of beads. Rex is more generous." Speaking of Rex, a 1938 *Times-Picayune* article reported that the King of Carnival's costume that year included a train composed of "a varicolored string of giant beads," emphasizing that beads had become as much a symbol of Mardi Gras as a crown, a mask, or a jester's hat. No one knows exactly why beads ascended to become the premier parade catchable in the 1930s. Maybe because tossing jewelry, albeit inexpensive glass jewelry, befit the faux royalty of the krewes. Maybe because beads can be immediately displayed around the neck, like parade trophies. Maybe just because beads are so satisfying to snag as they lasso through the air. To avoid tearful disappointments, New Orleans parents began hiding strands of beads from previous parades in their pockets to produce for their children in case said parents failed to catch any.

In the same decade that beads achieved emblematic status, a nationwide social development came about that would have an indirect but long-term effect on Carnival customs, including bead catching. In 1933, after thirteen years, Prohibition ended, making it no longer necessary for Mardi Gras royalty to pretend that their chalices were filled with grape juice or for ordinary folk to coyly conceal their flasks of smuggled brandy or Mason jars brimming with moonshine in their purses or coat pockets. Lifting one's mask for a snort was no longer a federal crime. In the twenty-first century, few places have drinking laws as lax as New Orleans. It would be impossible to openly imbibe on the curbs of the city's thoroughfares during parades while attempting to capture Mardi Gras beads if New Orleans's codes did not allow citizens and visitors alike to range freely while indulging in adult beverages. Consuming alcohol and participating in a Mardi Gras parade, either as a rider or a spectator, are not mutually dependent activities, of course. It is certainly possible to sling or snag beads while sober and to become less than sober without slinging or snagging beads. But in the minds of many, the activities are conjoined.

3

Bohemia, the Costume Jewelry Capital of the World

Bohemia is a rhomboid region of the Czech Republic smack-dab in the center of Europe. It is probably the source of the first glass beads tossed from Mardi Gras floats in late nineteenth-century New Orleans, for the simple reason that it was the source of most glass beads anywhere. At the top of Bohemia lies a town once called Gablonz, which was a beehive of bead production. In 1836, ten thousand people were involved in the manufacturing process. But don't imagine laborers marching off to some giant factory. According to Waltraud Neuwirth's straightforwardly titled 2011 article "Beads from Gablonz," the making of Bohemian glass beads was literally a cottage industry. Craftsmen and craftswomen gathered around home furnaces or in small mills, where they produced "scatter and embroidery beads, rassades and rocailles, macca and charlotte beads, drawn and blown beads, wound and mold-pressed beads, wax beads, baroque and craw beads, pound and string beads, spindles and spools, bugles, glass corals and glass garnets" by the billions, in innumerable shapes, including "spheres and olives, cubes and cylinders, rings and disks, spindles and spools, fruits and flowers."

Despite being exactingly handcrafted, Bohemian beads were always relatively inexpensive. According to a 1979 book titled *The Czech Bead Story* by Peter Francis Jr., the director of the Center for Bead Research in Lake Placid, New York, the growing efficiency of the Bohemian bead makers in the nineteenth century drove the quantity of exports ever upward, but the price of their handmade costume jewelry, known as *bijouterie,* steadily decreased. "By 1821 prices for glass beads had become significantly lower," wrote Francis, "and Bohemian business was booming, exporting something like 2,400,000,000 beads a year." The biggest customers were the twenty-four members of the United States, which included Louisiana by then, and Latin America. According to Neuwirth, prices dropped even further in the 1850s or 1860s, "after the invention of a mold that made it possible to blow a whole row of beads at once." So, at about the same time that Comus took to the streets in 1857, Bohemian bijouterie was dirt cheap. By the 1880s, strikes broke out among the glassmakers, as bead prices continued to sag.

Bohemia had long been a part of the Austro-Hungarian Empire. But at the end of World War I in 1918, it was blended with other territories to form a new, composite country called Czechoslovakia. This tells us that any string of glass beads marked with a label of Czechoslovakia has to have come from 1918 or later. Many of the bead

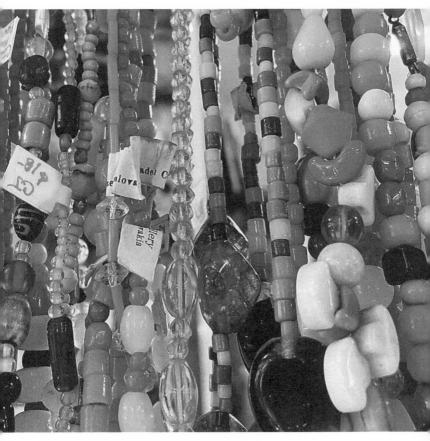

Czechoslovakian glass beads, like these found in a
Magazine Street curio shop, were immeasurably more
subtle and elegant than the plastic pearls that would
eventually replace them. Photo by Doug MacCash.

makers were of German lineage and, with the formation of Czecho-slovakia, they became an ethnic minority in the new country. But whatever alienation they may have felt apparently didn't stop them from churning out beads, beads, and more beads. By the mid-1920s, Czechoslovakia was the world's largest source of costume jewelry, and some of it may well have landed in the hands of New Orleanians. The "very pretty and extremely low in price" beads for "float maskers," sold by the Maison Blanche department store in 1922, could certainly have come from Czechoslovakia. Or not. To be clear, the possibility that Bohemian beads were tossed by riders in New Orleans Mardi Gras parades in the late nineteenth century and the first decades of the twentieth is logical, but unproven. And if Bohemian beads were tossed, how they were labeled is unknown. As of this writing, there are no antique strands of beads that can, with certainty, be traced to Carnival parades before 1918.

The Czech bead makers were known not only for their ability to mold glass, but for their ability to market it. They sent emissaries around the globe, searching for samples of indigenous beads that could be manufactured and offered for sale in those locales. Among their culturally specific products were Islamic prayer beads—which, to the wonderment of archaeologist Laurie Wilkie, were occasionally mixed in with the shipments of parade throws bound for New Orleans. One antique strand she examined included a medallion that praises Allah in Arabic, she said. Another strand of charming Czech beads in a New Orleans collection includes bean-sized glass sculptures of Santa Claus and miniature envelopes, probably meant to be letters beseeching the bringer of gifts. The strands of glistening, candy-colored, Czechoslovakian glass beads, of countless sizes and shapes, that became Mardi Gras throws were immeasurably more attractive than anything you might catch at a twenty-first-century Carnival parade. They were so beautifully made and varied that it's a wonder New Orleanians didn't wear them long after Ash Wednesday. But apparently, most didn't. As Wilkie points out, whenever you find antique Mardi Gras beads, they're liable to have a little paper label attached that says "Made in Czechoslovakia." Since the label is highly visible, it's unlikely the possessor of the beads ever wore them. Then, as now, Mardi Gras beads were a transient thrill, like the sparkle of fireworks.

The economic catastrophe that seized the world in the early 1930s naturally depressed Czech bead sales, which kindled civil unrest. In the throes of the worldwide economic depression, many ethnically German Czechs bought into the rhetoric of the fascist fanatic Adolf Hitler across the border, who vowed to bring them under the umbrella of the Third Reich. In his 1973 book *Czechoslovakia before Munich,* J. W. Bruegel states that representatives of the German Nationalist Party and the Nazi Party received roughly 400,000 votes in the 1925 and 1929 Czechoslovakian elections. An Associated Press story in the May 2, 1938, *Times-Picayune* reported that, during a May Day rally in the glass capital Gablonz, 40,000 residents turned out to hear Konrad Henlein, a gymnastics enthusiast and "Nazi leader of Czechoslovakia's 3,500,000 Germans." Henlein warned other nations not to support the government of Czechoslovakia in resisting Hitler's pledge to assimilate the region, at risk of war.

The Sudetenland, as the ethnically German zone had come to

be known, had a peculiar shape. It was a thin strip of territories that wrapped around the border of then Czechoslovakia like, well, a strand of beads. The US government warned the residents of the area that joining Hitler's Reich would lead to economic repercussions. An Associated Press story in the September 20, 1938, *States* foretold that the Czech collaborators could soon find themselves blacklisted by the United States in international trade. Experts said that many of Czechoslovakia's principal exports to the United States, "including textiles, glass, leather goods and cotton knit gloves would suffer by transfer of the Sudetenland to Germany."

But by October, European leaders had caved to Hitler, allowing him to absorb the Sudetenland into the Fatherland without a fight. When Hitler's storm troopers snapped up the slender territory, Czechoslovakia lost 86 percent of its glass industry. By allowing Hitler to waltz into the Sudetenland, diplomats hoped the raging racist would be mollified. But it didn't work out that way. In 1939 the Nazis invaded the rest of Czechoslovakia in what was the beginning of World War II in Europe.

Although the Sudetenland may have been a locus of glass production, German ancestry, and Nazi sympathy, that's not to say that all bead makers supported Hitler. Some surely rejected and resisted German influence and occupation as best they could. When the German Army seized Czechoslovakia, anti-Semitism became the law of the land. Many members of the Jewish faith and others in the occupied country were systematically murdered. According to the United States Holocaust Memorial Museum website, "the Germans and their collaborators killed approximately 263,000 Jews who had resided in the territory of the Czechoslovak Republic in 1938." An *Item* story in 1939 reported that the Nazi invasion immediately disrupted the bead trade. "As soon as Hitler took over Sudetenland, many Eastern importers of the Jewish faith cancelled contracts with Czechoslovak factories," said a bead wholesaler. "The only other place we can get beads from is Japan." But trade with Japan, which had invaded China in 1937, was also restricted. "The boycott has cut down that source too," the bead trader said. "Japan and the Czechs produced beads we could sell for 40 cents to 60 cents per gross" (roughly $7.50 to $11.25 in 2020 dollars). The Japanese would bomb the US fleet at Pearl Harbor in late 1941, and Germany declared war on Uncle Sam days later. For the following four years the United States would be in a bitter battle with the principal countries that controlled the bead trade.

World War II combat came closer to New Orleans than you might imagine. Nazi U-boats prowled beneath the waves of the Gulf of Mexico, torpedoing freighters that appeared in their periscopes. Some suspected that the submarines even slipped silently into the Mississippi River. Meanwhile, hundreds of thousands of American soldiers passed through the port on their way to the war in Europe, while hordes of German and Italian POWs were imprisoned at Camp Plauche a few miles upriver from the city. An abundance of Caribbean rum, coupled with a wartime shortage of other spirits, inspired mixologist and marketing genius Pat O'Brien to invent the high-octane Hurricane cocktail that is still served in a hurricane lamp–shaped glass and copiously consumed in the Vieux Carré to this day.

Speaking of booze shortages, some say that genius nautical designer Andrew Higgins's concept for the high-speed PT boats and landing craft that carried GIs onto the beaches of Normandy—contributing mightily to the eventual termination of the Third Reich—were inspired in part by his familiarity with the requirements of Louisiana rumrunners. The rum-running legend may or may not be true, but Higgins is indisputably a legendary character. Historian Stephen Ambrose, the cofounder of New Orleans's renowned National World War II Museum, said that Dwight D. Eisenhower, the supreme commander of the American forces in World War II, described Higgins as "the man who won the war for us." In an entertaining 2017 lecture, Ambrose described the Crescent City's wartime gestalt. He pointed out that the first New Orleanian to enlist in the Marines after Pearl Harbor was a dice dealer and that a hundred brothels sprang up in the City That Care Forgot in order to help servicemen momentarily forget their cares.

New Orleans officially suspended Carnival from 1942 to 1945. A *Times-Picayune* spread in February 1942, just two months after the bombing of the US fleet in Hawaii, featured a picture of what was going to be the paper's Mardi Gras souvenir edition crossed out with an emphatic black X. "New Orleans Knows How to Work as Well as Play," the page trumpets. "New Orleans has cancelled its biggest show to put on an even bigger show," meaning the world war.

During Carnival season 1943, an *Item* story previewed a Mardi Gras–style outdoor party scheduled to take place in the 800 block of Canal Street that year, with an emphasis on red, white, and blue over purple, green, and gold. The Higgins boat company band would play on the grandstand outside of D. H. Holmes, and anyone who had purchased a $1,000 war bond (which, adjusting for inflation, would cost almost $15,000 in 2020) would be allowed to watch the goings-on from the bleachers outside of the Boston Club. The photo at the top of the story depicted the "New Orleans Carnival king and queen" who had been redubbed "Uncle Sam and Miss Liberty." Some sort of procession may have been planned because the caption stated that the satin and sequined pair would "appear Tuesday night at the parade climaxing the Mardi Gras war bond and stamp drive." But, based on a follow-up report, there was no parade, just a spirited sing-along and the collection of more than $1 million for the war effort. There was no mention of wartime bead flinging, but if you thought that Mardi Gras beads couldn't possibly have played a role in World War II, you would be wrong.

Another 1943 story in the *Item,* titled "Mardi Gras Beads Head for Pacific," announces something called the "baubles for barter campaign," dreamed up by a General Galbreath of New Orleans's port of embarkation. "Nine barrels of jewelry for troop trading in the Pacific Islands were shipped to San Francisco today," the story states. The beads were apparently contributions from the stashes of parade-goers, collected at the D. H. Holmes department store, then bundled in two thousand bags with drawstrings by the American Women's Voluntary Services. The Lions Club paid the freight to the coast. Questions of the ultimate destination of the beads and details of their distribution surely popped into readers' heads then and now. But the story provides no further elucidation, nor does there seem to have been a follow-up.

New Orleans not only sent Mardi Gras beads to tropical climes, but it reversed the process. In 1946, a Carondelet Street importer advertised exotic alternatives to the usual costume jewelry. "Beads, Beads, Beads," the *States* ad read. "Now in stock for immediate delivery, the finest line of seashell necklaces . . . Very reasonable." The seashell beads, which included coconut shell accents, ranged in price from $1.50 to $5 per dozen (roughly $17 to $55 in 2020 terms). Who could have predicted that beads made from all-natural materials would become a health hazard? In 1949 certain strands of beads and bracelets that were tossed from floats were made from a cardinal-colored seed that contained one of the plant kingdom's deadliest toxins. "If one of the throws you caught during a Carnival parade is a bracelet with red and black beads, be careful, especially if there are children in the home," warned an *Item* story. A Loyola University pharmacy student named William Grace had, in fact, caught a bracelet made of the sinister Asian/Australian abrus seeds, known as rosary peas, during an Uptown parade. He astutely recognized the botanical hazard and alerted his professor, who sounded the alarm. Abrus seed jewelry had apparently been sold across the country, and a child in Wisconsin had died by sucking the seeds from a souvenir bracelet his mother had purchased in Florida.

The deadly scarlet seed beads were marketed at several Canal Street shops in preparation for Carnival parades, so it was difficult to tell how far and wide they'd flown. The Louisiana Department of Health prudently recommended that the poisonous seed beads be destroyed, but the agency couldn't take further action since the deadly seeds were not offered as a food or a drug and therefore lay beyond official jurisdiction. So the Department of Health relied on the shop owners to voluntarily take the remaining beads out of circulation. Two months later, a *States* story reported that eventually authorities succeeded in rounding up thousands of necklaces and bracelets in which the deadly abrus beads were used, some as far away as Hot Springs, Arkansas.

At least one New Orleanian took the appearance of the poisonous Mardi Gras beads as a sign. According to a March 19, 1949, *Item* advertisement, Reverend H. B. Roepe's Lenten radio sermon on station WNOE would address the hazards of accepting something for nothing. "How eagerly they strained to get their hands on a cheap string of beads, which were later reported to be poisonous if eaten," the reverend intoned to the post–Mardi Gras multitudes. "No doubt if the Kingdom of Heaven offered something cheap and glittering and poisonous, crowds would be storming its gates, crying God, throw me something! But because Christ offers free gifts of priceless value— forgiveness of sin, peace with God, power to overcome the devil and live for God, eternal life and joy beginning now—the world isn't interested. Are you blinded? On the streets of Mardi Gras you screamed and strained for worthless baubles. Will you not now cry to God, with repentant heart and with the same earnestness and longing?"

The reason krewes in post–World War II New Orleans had turned to seashell, coconut, and poisonous seed necklaces was probably because the costume jewelry industry that supplied glass beads before the war was in disarray. Not long after Hitler's Third Reich was defeated, Czechoslovakia became part of the Communist bloc. As the Iron Curtain dropped, the costume jewelry industry was collectivized and nationalized. But, according to Peter Francis in *The Czech Bead Story,* bead making wasn't a Cold War priority. By 1948, he wrote, "the industry was allowed to decline . . . because of questions concerning the appropriateness of the glass and costume jewelry industry." Maybe, Francis opined, "it was felt that beads and such trifles were of no crying necessity to the new socialist vision, or that a nation which desperately needed all of its strength to recover from the war would not waste its energy, capital, and manpower on such frivolities as personal ornaments."

In addition, a substantial percentage of the skilled labor was gone. After the war, most of the ethnically German Czechoslovakians, many of whom worked in the glass industry, were driven out of the country and resettled in Germany. Only those German Czechs who could prove that they had been anti-Nazi were allowed to stay. Eventually, some of the exiled glass craftsmen managed to rebuild their manufacturing operation across the border, founding a glass-making mill in a former German ammunitions plant in a town they redubbed New Gablonz, named after the old glass-manufacturing capital in Czechoslovakia. "By 1947, nearly a thousand Gablonzers had reestablished themselves in their traditional occupations, and the products of their industry were contributing to West Germany's export earnings," wrote historian R. M. Douglas in his sarcastically titled book *Orderly and Humane: The Expulsion of the Germans after the Second World War.* Somewhere along the line, Gablonz apparently became better known as Jablonec nad Nisou.

Despite the Communist government's presumed disdain for frivolities such as costume jewelry and the expulsion of many glass craftsmen to Germany, Czechoslovakia somehow continued to supply the Crescent City with bead necklaces for years to come. In a brief editorial in the 1950 Fat Tuesday issue of the *States,* an unnamed opinion writer warned that the bead trade would eventually get the Czechs in trouble with their masters in the Soviet Union. Since the USSR couldn't provide a market for luxuries such as glass bead necklaces, the Czechs were forced to "turn to consumer markets outside the [Iron] curtained countries," the editorialist argued. Eventually Czechoslovakia's commercial connections with the West would become more seductive than its political affinity with the Soviets. As the editorialist put it, "Trade, like blood, is thicker than water." The trouble was, the Soviets wouldn't be terribly tolerant of such a change in Czech economic orientation. The editorial, titled "Pity the Czech," turned out to be prescient. The Czechs would indeed become more westward leaning, and the Soviets would indeed yank the leash to bring them back into line. More about that later.

Bead archaeologist Laurie Wilkie said she stumbled upon a small treasure trove while scrolling through the selection of antique Mardi Gras beads available on eBay. Wilkie purchased eleven strands of antique beads that were all caught by a visitor to New Orleans in 1947, during the second Carnival after World War II. It's very rare to find a collection of beads that are known to come from the same exact year. The small selection is like a historical time capsule. Wilkie calls it an example of the "Pompeii Effect." Predictably, Wilkie's 1947 collection includes Czechoslovakian beads, but unexpectedly it also includes beads that, according to their labels, were made in the "Occupied Germany U.S. Zone." These might have been examples of bijouterie produced by exiled German Czechs who had swiftly reentered the international costume jewelry trade. Or they might have been made by the enclave of long-established but less well known German glass makers in Bavaria. German-made Carnival beads are exceptionally scarce—so much so that even Carnival aficionados have rarely heard of them—but Wilkie says the ones she found aren't terribly impressive otherwise. She describes them as "minimalist Mardi Gras strands," composed of simple green and white, round and oval shapes.

Finally, Wilkie's eBay purchase includes beads that were made in postwar Japan, where General Douglas MacArthur decreed that all exports from the defeated island nation were to be marked "Made in Occupied Japan," from 1945 until 1952. The earliest strands of postwar Japanese beads were composed of tiny blown glass orbs, as light-weight, hollow, and shiny as miniature Christmas tree ornaments. Later, the Japanese bead makers added glass tubes, as slender as macaroni, to their New Orleans–bound necklaces. Strands of rice beads were also eventually available, which, as the name implies, were delicate strings of tiny grain-like ovals. According to Wilkie, the first Japanese Mardi Gras beads were amber, green, blue, clear, gold, or silver, but eventually other colors entered the mix. An advertisement in the *States* in 1953 calls the attention of krewe members to "Long Jap Glass Beads" for sale for $1.60 per gross (adjusted for inflation, about $15.50 in today's dollars) at a Camp Street business called Mann's. Long Japanese rice beads sold for 65 cents per gross ($6.33 in 2020 dollars). It's ironic that glass beads tossed to patriotic Crescent City crowds in the second Carnival after World War II were made by former or future avowed enemies of the good ol' USA: Germany, Japan, and communist Czechoslovakia.

Indian glass bead necklaces eventually entered the Mardi Gras throw trade, but exactly when is unknown. In his book *Beads of the World,* bead maven Peter Francis Jr. explains that, though there were centuries-old bead-making traditions in India already, "in 1942 a Czech couple went to [the city of] Benares to teach the locals how to make glass." There, they established a glass-making school that helped foster an industry. A 1968 advertisement in the *Times-Picayune* calls the attention of float riders to "an immense shipment of glass beads from India" imported by the Trager Company. The throws were said to be superior to beads made in other "exotic" places. According to the ad, which was designed to resemble a news story, the Trager employees remarked: "They're extra heavy and can't be resisted."

In 1958, ten years after Czechoslovakia had become a Soviet satellite, the government officially began backing the country's glass industry, presumably seeking a further infusion of capitalist cash. Shipments of Czech beads to the Crescent City may have increased. An enterprising flooring supplier named Sam Cimino, who sold Mardi Gras beads on the side, imported over twenty thousand gross of Czechoslovakian beads in 1958, according to an advertisement in the *Times-Picayune.* Naturally, not everyone approved of the preponderance of communist-made Mardi Gras beads on the streets of decidedly anti-red New Orleans. During the 1964 Carnival season, a letter to the editor of the *States Item* was titled "Sell to Commies, But Don't Buy, She Says." In it, Mrs. Frederick James of Westwego advocated that, since citizens were continuously threatened with atomic annihilation by communists, they should not buy their beads. "I believe that buying anything from a Communist country is unnecessary and unwarranted," James wrote. "Why give five cents of American money to help keep the arms race going?"

Anti-Soviet sentiment ran deep in Cold War New Orleans, yet there were opposing points of view. In the same year that Mrs. Frederick James encouraged New Orleanians to boycott Czech Carnival beads, *States Item* columnist Pie Dufour defended their importation. Dufour pointed out that the United States, and particularly New Orleans, came out way ahead in the bargain. "Consider the wide differential in our foreign trade with Czechoslovakia here in New Orleans," Dufour wrote, "with $733,000 worth of goods going out of our port and only $138,000 worth coming in." If New Orleans cancelled imports from Czechoslovakia and the Czechs retaliated, "Who'd be the material loser," Dufour asked. Riders preferred robust Czech beads over lighter-weight Japanese beads, he wrote, and he said he hoped that throw importers would continue to make them available. "Surely I know that Czechoslovakia is an Iron Curtain country, but the United States trades with Russia doesn't it," Dufour asked, cheekily adding that there was nothing more "Iron Curtainish" than the Soviet Union. "Those who feel squeamish about using Iron Curtain country beads certainly have every right not to buy them," Dufour continued. "But those American citizens who feel that they have the right to keep step with their government in the matter of foreign trade should also have the right to buy Czech beads if they wish."

Unknown to Dufour, or anyone else in New Orleans for that matter, there might have been a humanitarian reason not to buy Communist Czechoslovakian beads. According to one source, the totalitarian

Czech government forced political prisoners to produce some of its exported bijouterie. The headline of a 1988 story in the *Observer,* a London newspaper, read "Scandal of Slave Labour in Prison's Glass-works." In the exposé, reporter John Sweeney described a London shop owner who felt "extremely uncomfortable" when she was told that the Czech beads she offered for sale might have been made by inmate labor. The revelation was delivered by a visitor to the shop named Jaroslav Javorsky, who claimed to have been locked up in the enormous Bohemian prison for having helped his girlfriend escape the Eastern Bloc. "The prisoners are worked ferociously hard," Sweeney wrote. "Javorsky produced 30 to 40 kilograms [about 66 to 88 pounds] of glass beads a day. Another section of the prison assembled necklaces in the monastery church."

In a 1991 pamphlet called *The Margaretologist,* published by the Center for Bead Research, aforementioned costume jewelry authority Peter Francis Jr. suggests that Mr. Sweeney's and/or his source might have exaggerated the situation. According to Francis's own unnamed contacts in the bead trade, only "a rather tiny percentage of the total production of Czech beads are made by prison labor." And anyway, "how could Czech beads be imported to the United States," Francis asked. "For a century there has been a law in the U.S. that forbids the importation of goods produced by convict, forced, or indentured labor," he wrote. If prisoner-produced beads had entered the United States, Francis concluded, they were probably "slipped into lots coming from other producers, and thus enter the market surreptitiously."

It's disturbing to consider that what Sweeney called "cheap imitation jewelry" made by Czech dissidents "in conditions little better than slave labour," in "the "most severe" correctional establishment in Czechoslovakia, may have fallen into the hands of beseeching Crescent City children. Thankfully, it's hard to be sure it ever really happened. For one thing, Mr. Sweeney allowed that not all Czech glassware was "prison-made." And since the story doesn't say exactly when the prison bead-production system began, it's hard to say if the forced labor coincided with Czechoslovakian bead tossing in New Orleans in the late 1950s and 1960s. By the 1970s, glass beads were going out of style, whether political prisoners produced them or not. An advertisement in a 1953 edition of the *States* offers a variety of Carnival beads, including "Beautiful heavy bead necklaces, imported from Europe at the unbelievable price of $8 per gross." The ad makes it clear that these unbelievably priced beads are "NOT PLASTIC"—which, of course, tells us that the era of plastic beads had begun.

4

The Booming
Bead Business

Visit a New Orleans curio shop, and you're liable to find an array of Czechoslovakian and Japanese glass Mardi Gras beads that date from the middle decades of the twentieth century. Most of the antique necklaces available today are just big enough to stretch around a slender neck. They are eye-catching, cast in innumerable colors from primaries to pastels, to marbled earth tones, yet they are not gaudy. Composed of glass ovals, diamonds, cylinders, cubes, and other shapes of various sizes and sequences, they are as individual as fingerprints. They are inexpensive, sometimes under ten dollars per strand, but precious.

Czech bead makers used an array of compounds and minerals to color the beads bound for far-away Carnival parades. Starting in the nineteenth century, powdered uranium oxide was part of their palette. They employed the mineral to produce a translucent, chartreuse-hued glass that came to be called Vaseline glass, because it matched the color of petroleum jelly. It doesn't seem to have troubled anyone that the Vaseline glass was mildly radioactive.

Yes, radioactive. Shine an ultraviolet light on a collection of antique glass Mardi Gras beads and chances are, a strand or two might glow with an eerie green luminescence right out of a science fiction movie. Antique dealers sometimes create small blacklight cabinets to display vintage glowing glass objects. Collectors consider the vast majority of the uranium wine cups, light sconces, sugar bowls, and Mardi Gras beads that were produced during the Vaseline glass heyday to be harmless. The fad faded during the Cold War, as rival governments amassed the glowing mineral to make atomic bombs.

Despite their beauty, to this day, mid-century glass beads are remembered as much for their functional flaws as their appearance. If two parade-goers got hold of a necklace simultaneously, the string that bound them was sure to break, sending the glass beads scattering under the feet of the mules, marching bands, and flambeaux. Since glass is a relatively heavy material, larger strands of glass beads flew through the winter air with enough velocity to sting the knuckles or bridge of the nose, or worse. And occasionally the glass elements—especially the extraordinarily thin Japanese glass elements—snapped, causing minor cuts.

In 1940, the *States* reported that "Mrs. Crawford H. Ellis, wife of a former king of the Carnival, had a front tooth broken when she eagerly grasped for a string of beads from a float and the beads struck her squarely in the face." In 1949, a *Times-Picayune* ad, possibly penned by a personal injury attorney, sought "witnesses to accident and eye injury of pedestrian from thrown beads near Panola [Street], Krewe of Carrollton parade, Sunday, Feb. 20." In a letter to the editor of the *Times-Picayune* in 1949, a so-called A.B. complained, "Three out of five strings of beads get broken" and precipitated injuries both directly and incidentally. "One trinket hit a friend of mine in the neck with such force she still had a pain in the neck the day after," A.B. wrote. "A group of rough-necks tackled her from all directions to get the worthless piece of trash." A.B. endorsed eliminating "throwouts"—a bygone term that has since been shortened to "throws"—entirely so that "people then can really enjoy the beauty of the shimmering floats without being pummeled, shoved and stomped upon."

In 1954, while attending the Carrollton parade in the Gallier Hall grandstands, Mayor deLesseps "Chep" Morrison "cut his hand while snagging a string of beads." On Mardi Gras morning during the same year, the mayor's wife, Corrine, was also injured. Mrs. Morrison had collected a "whole armload of beads" on behalf of her children. But her success did not come without a price. "To get these," she bravely recounted, "I was hit in the forehead with some beads and was almost knocked out. It really hurt and I wanted to cry, but I didn't want to cry either, so I managed not to." Some say that injuries from glass beads became such a public safety issue that they were eventually banned, but that probably isn't so. "Local legend suggests that an ordinance was passed against glass beads, because of the danger of them breaking in crowds as they were thrown, but there is no evidence of any such local restrictions," wrote Carnival historian Lissa Capo in her 2011 University of New Orleans M.A. thesis, "Throw me Something Mister: The History of Carnival Throws in New Orleans." Rather, Capo wrote, it is likely "the development of plastic, a sturdier and cheaper substitute, prompted the change." Plus, there was yet more political turmoil in Czechoslovakia. After years of dissatisfaction, in 1968 the Czechs pushed away from the Soviet empire, for a brief historical moment known as the Prague Spring. In a few months, convoys of Soviet tanks rolled across the border like the Germans had thirty years earlier to nip springtime in the bud.

The gradual disappearance of glass beads didn't eliminate the possibility of injuries from Carnival throws, as anyone who's been zapped across the face on a cold winter day with a long strand of plastic pearls can testify. In 1979, the Louisiana state legislature passed a bill that would make it difficult for someone injured by beads or other throws to sue Carnival krewes or individual riders. As the author of Revised Statute 9:2796 put it, "Any person who is attending or participating in one of the organized parades of floats, assumes the risk of being struck by any missile whatsoever which has been traditionally thrown, tossed, or hurled by members of the krewe or organization." The list of missiles in the liability limiting legislation included beads, cups, coconuts, doubloons, and any other sorts of Carnival throws. It's likely that the 1979 law was a factor in the continued enlargement of beads, which became heftier and heftier in the decades that followed. Bobby Hjortsberg, who is both an attorney and the captain of the Krewe of Freret, said that parade-goers can still sue krewes, if they believe they were deliberately injured by a float rider, or due to gross negligence. Hjortsberg said that, limited liability or not, the leaders of the Freret parade instruct riders to behave responsibly. "We tell people, 'Use your common sense,'" he said. "Don't throw full bags of beads overhand." In short, Hjortsberg said, parade-riders

The seemingly endless Krewe of Elks Orleans truck parade is a bead-catching paradise for kids and adults alike. Photo by Michael DeMocker, NOLA.com | *The Times-Picayune,* 2017, Capital City Press/Georges Media Group, Baton Rouge, LA.

are told: "Don't be assholes." Without the protection provided by the law, he pointed out, parades might not exist as we know them. "If you put us in a situation where we could get sued," he said, "it would probably make it impossible to get insurance." As it stands, he said, the Krewe of Freret pays Lloyd's of London roughly $10,000 for three hours of liability insurance.

Roland Barthes was one of the modern era's most revered cultural observers. The French philosopher saw the world as a never-ending crossword puzzle, where the definitions of words overlapped and interlocked in ways we intend and ways we never imagined. Everything, in Barthes's view, meant something. So he wrote about everything, from pro wrestling to soap powder to Balzac's novel about an alluring androgynous actress. In 1957, he published an essay about the substance that would soon rise above all other manufacturing materials in a tone so highbrow it sounds a little tongue-in-cheek. And maybe it was. In his essay "Plastic," Barthes mythologizes the material, pointing out that various types of plastic sound like they were named for Greek shepherds: Polystyrene, Phenplast, Polyvinyl, and Polyethylene. The making of plastic, he wrote, is like alchemy, "a magical operation par excellence" with "the raw substance" at one end and "the perfect human object" at the other. "Plastic's quick-change talent is total," he wrote, "it can form pails as well as jewels." Plus, he pointed out, it is in the ability to perform such astonishing transformations "that man measures his power."

Barthes surely never imagined it, but his description of the powers of plastic accidentally defined the ethos of the Carnival throwing game to a T. Where else do plastic jewels more clearly become the measure of human power? And if plastic is a symbolic measure of power, then the most powerful parading organization bar none is the Krewe of Endymion, which, like so many plastics, is named after an obscure Greek shepherd. Or so it would seem. The truth is, the Krewe of Endymion was named for a racehorse that once galloped at the New Orleans Fair Grounds track, which is near the original starting spot of the parade that first rolled in 1967. The horse was named for the obscure Greek shepherd. But whether the parade is named for a sheepherder or a horse, the hailstorm of plastic jewels, toys, and trinkets hurled by the all-male Endymion riders is nothing short of Olympian. The krewe's motto is "Throw Until It Hurts."

Dan Kelly, the president of the Krewe of Endymion, said that when he joined the organization in 1970, each of the 165 riders climbed aboard his assigned float equipped with 100 to 150 pounds of throws. In 2020, each of the 3,200 male riders stands amidst a stash of 500 pounds of imported treasure. In 1970, Kelly recalled, the average length of a plastic pearl necklace was 24 to 33 inches long, with maybe a few choice 42-inchers in the mix. Now the beads range from 33 inches to an astonishing ten feet in length. In 1970, beads cost about two cents per strand. In 2020, the smallest beads cost five cents, with the preferred, hand-strung beads running from $1.50 to $10 per strand. In 1970, Endymion might have spent $150,000 to $200,000 on throws. In 2020, the krewe spent between $1 million and $1.5 million.

Kelly is not just the president of New Orleans's most bead-happy krewe, he is the big dog of Crescent City Carnival throw importers. His Beads by the Dozen retail showroom, in a New Orleans suburb called Harahan, is like a small grocery store where cart-pushing shoppers circulate through the aisles, selecting from hundreds and hundreds of varieties of beads, as well as everything from plastic flying disks to feather boas. It is a wonderland of the irredeemably impractical and irrelevant. Kelly said he became acquainted with the bead business when he volunteered to store Endymion throws for free in a warehouse owned by his family, thereby saving the organization thousands. Next, he tagged along with the krewe's bead supplier Ernie Kruttschnitt to Hong Kong, just to lay eyes on the Asian end of the bead importation trade. Kelly's said that the Hong Kong costume jewelry factories were wonderments, with sixty to eighty women operating bead-molding machines on one floor and a similar number of women stringing the beads into necklaces on another. Kelly said he doubts that the factory workers understood the celebration they were contributing to. More than once, he said, Chinese sales representatives indelicately advised him that the combination of purple, green, and gold colors that he seemingly adores is, well, ugly. When Kruttschnitt passed away, Kelly took over the bead importation company. "It's become a hell of a business," he said.

In 2020, Kelly said he'd guess the riders in the roughly fifty parades in the New Orleans area spend $30 million to $40 million on throws. Maybe even $50 million The bead factories eventually moved from Hong Kong to inland China, Kelly said. He usually spends part of each spring touring the trinket trade shows in the People's Republic, searching for new novelties to satisfy the throw-me-something Misters and Missuses back in New Orleans. Though he's profited handsomely over the years, Kelly said he's always provided Endymion's beads at cost, which helps explain Endymion's legendary munificence.

Plastic beads may have come on the Carnival scene as early as the 1950s, but, based on the collective memory of ageing parade-goers, it wasn't until the late 1960s that they became a major part of the "catch." The earliest plastic beads from Hong Kong didn't look much different from the Czech glass beads they would eventually replace. Based on examples found in Crescent City curio stores, most were collar-length necklaces, composed of variously shaped, sized, and colored beads, hand-strung on a white thread and looped together with a simple clasp. From a fashion point of view, they might have been a touch tackier than their glass counterparts, but to those shouting "throw me something mister" along the parade routes, they were perfectly acceptable. The next big development was something called molded-on-string beads (or sometimes molded-on-thread) beads. As the name suggests, these were beads produced by machines that formed plastic orbs onto a sturdy, synthetic string. MOS beads, as they are known in the trade, immediately solved the problem of the scattering of loose beads from broken strands. Early versions of MOS beads were choker-length, lightweight strings of pastel-hued, translucent balls, not much larger than BBs, that were held together with pliable, plastic, ball-and-socket clasps. Parade-goers of a certain age probably recall the peculiar popping sound when the strands were unclasped and removed at the end of the night. The need for clasps of any kind was eliminated when manufacturers began producing longer "ropes" of MOS beads that easily slipped over an adult's head. Many of those ropes were composed of metallic orbs about the size of peas. Some of the beads were faceted, like tiny disco balls. Eventually MOS beads appeared in all shapes, including hearts, lentils, pinecones, barrels, twists, arrow heads and—you name it.

Above all other reasons for the shift to plastic beads was the cost. Czech and Japanese beads were cheap, but Hong Kong beads were cheaper. In 1966, Sam "Mr. Cut Rate" Cimino's business, Cut Rate Lino-leum, sold Czech beads for $4.50 per gross and plastic beads for $3.00 per gross. Allowing for inflation, that would be $36 and $24 respec-tively in today's dollars, or 25 cents per strand for glass beads and 16 cents for plastic. Based on Cimino's ad in the *Times-Picayune,* there's no way of comparing the relative quality of the glass and plastic prod-ucts, but on its face, parade-riders who bought plastic beads could count on the same number of tosses for two-thirds the price of glass. By the late 1970s, plastic had almost entirely replaced its competitors.

Life-long Mardi Gras enthusiast Jimmy Clark said he remembers catching glass beads during Carnival parades in the French Quarter when he was a kid in the 1950s. "You didn't see a lot of them," he said of the Czech and Japanese necklaces. "If I went home with one or two strands, I'd be happy. You didn't come home with bags and bags full, like you do today." Once in a while, he said, he'd receive a nick on the finger from a sharp edge, but it was never serious. As a teenager, Clark began writing consumer reviews of Carnival parades, using a rigorous list of criteria. In the pages of community newspapers, he rated the quality of the float decoration, the speed of the parade, the number of bands, and other details. Writing parade reviews was never terribly lucrative, but when Clark got into the throw importation business in the late 1970s, his passion for Carnival paid off. Clark said that the low price and practicalities of plastic manufacturing certainly set the stage for the bead boom of the late twentieth and twenty-first centuries. But he believes the single most significant cause for bead inflation had nothing to do with beads at all; it was inspired by the advent of another favorite throw.

In 1960 the King of Carnival began minting his own money. For the first time that year, in addition to beads and toys, Mardi Gras morning crowds scrambled to catch glinting aluminum coins with the profile of Rex on one side and the words "Pro Bono Publico" (for the public good) on the other. The Zulu Social Aid and Pleasure Club had been the source of signature coconuts since at least the 1920s. But Clark said that Rex doubloons, as they were dubbed, are remembered as the first branded Mardi Gras throws manufactured by a parading organization. The truth is, Clark said, riders in the bygone Grela parade tossed wooden nickels imprinted with the Krewe of Grela logo three days before the debut of Rex doubloons, but the nickels have been mostly lost to history. The shiny Rex coinage, on the other hand, instantly became a prime Carnival collectible. Before doubloons, Clark explained, parade-goers would reach Ash Wednesday with heaps of booty, but they mostly "wouldn't have known which thing came from which parade." The Rex doubloons were unmistakably a souvenir of that specific event. Other krewes soon followed Rex's lead, minting Carnival coins of their own. Soon, the krewes began dating their doubloons and altering the images on the faces of the faux coins. In just a few years, there was such a wide range of krewe currency that generations of doubloon numismatists sprang up to covet and catalog them.

According to Clark, the reason doubloons sped up the arms race is because they weren't just symbolic money; they represented real money for the parading organizations. "Before doubloons," he said, "the income of krewes was limited to dues, to pay for everything, including the parades and balls." The riders of the era bought their throws from retailers, so those purchases didn't add any cash to the krewes' coffers. But doubloons were commissioned by the various parading groups and sold to members at a profit. "The doubloons were an opportunity for throws to make money," Clark said. "They cost three cents and the captains sold them for five cents [to riders] to benefit the krewes." From then on, Clark said, branded throws, including plastic drinking cups, custom-made plush toys, plastic flying disks, and branded beads helped pay the parading organizations' annual bills. "You could only buy krewe items from the krewe," Clark said. Importers instructed manufacturers to produce throws to the krewes' specification, which would be sold exclusively to the members after a markup. For example, Clark said, a krewe captain might buy prepackaged mixtures of throws, including branded items, from an importer for $200 each and sell them for $300 to members. "It didn't take long for captains to realize they had a captive market," he said. And there were more krewe captains than ever.

According to Clark, more new parading organizations popped up in the 1960s and 1970s than in the entire previous history of Carnival. That blossoming of new krewes nurtured a burgeoning crop of throw importers and retailers across the region. Cut Rate Carnival Novelties (formerly Cut Rate Linoleum) and Jefferson Variety Store, which were already established before the boom, were joined by K-International, Oriental Merchandise, Carnival Mart, Westside Carnival Mart, Deep South Imports, TJ Carnival Supplies, Broadmoor Carnival Novelties, and Accent Annex (which would eventually have a chain of ten locations). Clark said that even the once-ubiquitous, now-defunct Schwegmann's grocery store chain added Mardi Gras beads and other throws to their inventory.

New to the business in 1978, Clark set out to produce a new, more practical type of throw—krewe-branded coasters—that would remain useful long after the parade had passed. At first, he considered using a manufacturer in Pennsylvania to produce the coasters, but a krewe captain advised him that he could save money by taking his business to Asia. "He might as well have said, 'You could get these coasters made on the moon,'" Clark recalled. "You could have asked a ten-year-old kid on the street and he would know as much about importing as I did." But, thanks to contacts Clark made through the Hong Kong Trade Development Council in Chicago, it wasn't long before trucks were dropping off enormous shipping containers full of throws in his front yard. "I'm not sure to this day where the factories were," he said. By the time he sold his J. Clark Promotions import company to Dan Kelly in 2009, he was receiving seventy-five containers of throws from Asia and providing $4 million to $5 million in beads and baubles to float riders each season. Kelly's Beads by the Dozen and a supplier called Plush Appeal, a purveyor of stuffed toys to state fairs and amusement parks, would eventually come to dominate the marketplace.

Uncle Sam had a role in stimulating the bead importation business. "The U.S. Customs Service once subjected Mardi Gras beads to a duty of between 11 percent and 27.5 percent," wrote *Times-Picayune* business reporter Stewart Yerton in a 1999 story, "but in 1989, under a special provision of the U.S. Congress, the duty was eliminated on plastic bead necklaces costing less than 30 cents per dozen." In 1995, Washington sweetened the deal further, granting duty-free status to practically all Mardi Gras beads. A spasm of concern rippled among bead importers and float riders in August 2019 when President Donald Trump threatened to impose a 10 percent tariff on all imports from China, which would have upped the cost of most Carnival throws. Fortunately, for all participants in the throwing game, the president's plan didn't materialize.

As the Mardi Gras bead market grew over the decades, so did the beads. "Size matters," wrote *Times-Picayune* editor Karen Taylor Gist in a column during Carnival 2008. "I've been here long enough to recall the cheapie, post-glass-era but pre-long-bead strands that barely fit over your head. I dove for them like they were gold. Now, 33-inchers are about the shortest sold, and even they've become like the parsley on your dinner plate: A nice touch of color to fill an empty spot, but totally dispensable. Ground fodder. Keepers have to be at least 48 inches (that's to the bikini line). And even then, the size of the individual bead can make or break the desirability rating. . . . Length has to hit 60 inches (crotch-length) to be a sure thing for saving." The phenomenon of ever-elongating beads was just one of three Carnival developments that sprouted in the 1970s and continued unabated into the present. There was also the debut of medallions, information-bearing disks that when attached to a strand of Mardi Gras beads, converted the faux jewelry into the dangling equivalent of a printed T-shirt. At first medallion beads merely identified the krewe that threw them, but eventually they came to be mini-billboards for corporate advertisements, pro sports boosterism, political messages, and social causes. But before the chapter on medallion beads comes the chapter about ritual disrobement.

5

Show Me Something, Mister . . . or Miss

It is impossible to catalog the cultural implications of Carnival beads without casting our gaze at a relatively minor phenomenon that has lent an exaggerated sense of sexuality to the "throwing game." We are, of course, talking about flashing for beads. From Honolulu, Hawaii, to Bar-Harbor, Maine; from Anchorage, Alaska, to Laredo, Texas, absolutely everyone knows that, during New Orleans's Carnival, some women peel up their T-shirts to reveal their breasts and some men slide down their jeans to expose their buttocks and genitalia in exchange for plastic necklaces. These inebriated acts of abandon, tolerated if not condoned by the Crescent City's constabulary, bolster New Orleans's magnetically unruly mystique. But according to sociology professor Dr. John C. Kilburn of Texas A&M International University in the aforementioned Laredo, Texas, the majority of those baring themselves for beads on the streets of New Orleans aren't New Orleanians. "Most of the people are outsiders," Kilburn said. "They say

Despite New Orleans's anything-goes reputation, by the
late 1990s, flashing for beads was perceived as a problem
by the civic leaders of the City That Care Forgot. This photo
is from the Hermes parade in 1995. Photo by Mitchel L.
Osborne. Courtesy of The Historic New Orleans Collection,
acc. no. 2007.0001.78.

'I'm here, what the heck, why not?'" It makes sense, he said. Locals might recognize one another in the compromising act, while tourists remain cloaked in anonymity. Kilburn is one of the world's authorities on flashing for beads. Back in the early 1990s, when he was a grad student in the Sociology Department at Louisiana State University, he helped Professor Wesley Shrum study the phenomenon. Kilburn and Shrum shot thirty-one hours of video tape that captured 1,492 instances of bead/breast/buttocks negotiations. The vast majority of requests to swap beads for forbidden glimpses of anatomy were met with the answer "no," Kilburn said. But sometimes, deals were struck before his lens.

Kilburn said that most Vieux Carré flashing took place after dark on Bourbon Street in the few days leading to Fat Tuesday. Instances of exhibitionism occurred on wrought iron–wrapped balconies and in the grimy street below. Not surprisingly, his research demonstrated that those on the balconies seemed to be in command of the beads-for-exposure transactions, while those in the street were supplicants. The balcony is "a stage where lots of people can see you," Kilburn said, and the flashers on the elevated balconies were clearly the "elite performers." Chants such as "Show your tits" or "Show your dicks" rang out as expectant crowds gathered beneath balconies to watch the ad hoc strip shows, he recalled. Those willing to disrobe, however briefly, on the balconies were able to command that they receive beads tossed from the street below before they exposed themselves, while those in the street were made to reveal themselves before receiving their rewards from above. Often, Kilburn said, flashers would barter with bead-bearers, insisting on certain premium strands. They'd say

"No, not those . . . I want THOSE," Kilburn recalled. An unspoken code of the exchanges kept the participants at a safe distance, Kilburn said. Interactions between exhibitionists and exhibitionees at street level were rare. "If you violated the rules of the game, it could become creepy, could become criminal," he surmised.

Nudity was already ingrained in the French Quarter milieu, with risqué Carnival costumes dating back more than a century, decades-old Bourbon Street strip clubs, and most recently, gay discos where various degrees of exhibitionism sometimes escaped the dance floor onto the balconies. Through most of the twentieth century, Carnival parades plied the narrow streets of the French Quarter, scattering beads and baubles as they rattled along. But when the parades were detoured around the city's oldest neighborhood in 1973, there seems to have been a residual craving to catch beads. Balcony denizens tossed trinkets to passersby in the street below, as if they were riders on a stationary float. This is the tinder pile of social confluences in which flashing would flare up. In searching for the spark that first ignited the phenomenon, Kilburn said that he and Shrum met two participants in a legendary Carnival party in 1976 in which nudists cavorted on the balcony of an apartment at 933 Royal Street. At first, the nudists challenged the crowd below to join them in disrobing. Somewhere along the line, somebody exchanged a peek at his or her private parts in exchange for Carnival throws and a culturally defining tradition was born. At least that seemed to be the beads-for-body-parts genesis story.

A quarter-century after Shrum and Kilburn concluded their French Quarter study, a sixty-five-year-old artist living in Harper, Texas, came forward to put a finer point on the origin of the eyebrow-raising custom. Ann Lyneah Curtis said that, to the best of her knowledge, she pioneered the practice. The notorious 1976 ground zero balcony party had taken place at the second-story apartment she shared with her boyfriend. Curtis, who was nineteen at the time, takes credit for having hung out a sign that said "Show Your Tits" to help entice passersby to flash. A friend, she said, made a similar sign suggesting that males expose their genitals. "We realized we could probably get them to entertain us," she said. Though Curtis said she does not recall exposing herself from the balcony that day, she had done so earlier in the morning on Canal Street.

Curtis, a Jackson Square portrait artist who had dabbled in nude modeling and topless dancing, said she found herself sitting on a friend's shoulders competing for beads tossed from Rex parade floats. It dawned on her, she said, that she could draw particular attention to herself by stretching down the top of her shirt to give float riders a glimpse of what lay beneath. "I figured that would be the best way to get the most beads." Curtis said she didn't see anyone else doing it and wasn't reprimanded by the police. Feminism, she said, wasn't on her radar at the time, but she didn't feel exploited by the float riders. "I was in control of the situation, definitely," she said. "I was comfortable in my own skin and wasn't afraid of showing it."

After a story revealing Curtis's long-ago exploits appeared in the *Times-Picayune* in 2020, several readers commented that the flashing phenomenon had popped up before 1976, certainly in the early 1970s and maybe as far back as the 1950s. Professor Shrum said that he wouldn't argue. "There was probably not one single origin" of the erotic custom, he said. Sociologically speaking, French Quarter flashing was probably a manifestation of the general rebellious nature of the patchouli-oiled, tie-died, freak-flag era. "There were probably multiple simultaneous discoveries" as uninhibited revelers expressed their liberty for all the world to see. After all, "it was the 'Easy Rider' generation," Shrum said, "the free love and drugs generation. The idea of nudity expressed freedom from exploitation, from patriarchy, from traditional institutional restraints."

The 1969 film *Easy Rider* is a low-budget, counterculture buddy movie in which the ill-fated heroes Billy, played by Dennis Hopper, and Wyatt, played by Peter Fonda, set out on a cross-country trip to the Mardi Gras atop glittering motorcycles. The theme of the film is a quest for ineffable freedom, via the open road, long hair, weed, wine, and cavorting with the Carnival crowd in New Orleans. In one of the most memorable scenes, Billy and Wyatt, accompanied by two pros-titutes, visit one of New Orleans's picturesquely creepy above-ground cemeteries at the edge of the French Quarter. The quartet consumes psychedelic drugs to better commune with the crumbling tombs and statuary. The drugs have a nightmarish effect, as illustrated by untra-ditional camera work. Wyatt weeps. One of the call girls gets naked.

Yes, flashing for beads may have simply been an expression of the "Born to Be Wild" era's uninhibitedness. But Shrum said there's a deeper, socioeconomic implication as well. By flashing for beads, he said, "we figured out how to perfectly symbolize the free market society." During conventional parades, he pointed out, ersatz kings, queens, and their courts symbolically share their great wealth by toss-ing faux treasure to their adoring subjects in the street below. Which,

Shrum pointed out, is the old, medieval system of noblesse oblige. Flashing, on the other hand, requires no subservient gratitude. It is a simple exchange of goods for services rendered. "We converted the largesse of the elite," he said, "to a symbolic reenactment of the Capitalist system." In that way, he said, flashing for beads "symbolized our commitment to a moral order." In a 1999 *Times-Picayune* story, business writer Stewart Yerton delightedly describes the fleshy capitalism that Shrum said underlies the flashing custom. "Bourbon Street is the Wall Street of the bead trading world," Yerton wrote. "On Thursday night, revelers at the Royal Sonesta Hotel stood on a corner balcony at Bourbon and Conti and dangled beads like fishing worms. Clutches of tourists gathered underneath, calling to the balconies like raunchy Romeos. In one 10-minute span, one man dropped his pants and offered a frontal view, another showed a full moon and a woman lifted her striped T-shirt. Beads rained on them." Yerton interviewed two young men—Fabio Mangione and Mark Kalinowski of New Haven, Connecticut—who succinctly defined the supply side of the economic equation. "If you've got no beads being a guy, you've got no power," Kalinowski explained. "The more beads you got the more power you got." April Ballesteros, an unrepentant flasher, described the demand side of the exchange. It was, she said, the adrenaline rush and the attention that motivated her, not the beads.

Shrum said that the days when visitors to the Crescent City Carnival could count on anonymity as they exposed body parts in exchange for plastic have passed since he and Kilburn conducted their studies in the early 1990s. Thanks to videos and photos that can be readily disseminated via social media posts, what happens in New Orleans certainly does not stay in New Orleans anymore. By the time many an erstwhile exhibitionist drives back to Birmingham or Fort Worth, with splendid beads dangling from their necks and rearview mirrors, their exploits may be well known among their Facebook followers. However, Shrum said, the practice of flashing for beads in the so-called Big Easy is so broadly known that it's probably not viewed as deviant, even by viewers far, far from the balconies of the Vieux Carré. Shrum said that, in the years since his 1990s research, he's also come to believe that flashing by New Orleans natives is more common than he once believed. Some of his Crescent City–born students have assured him that plenty of locals lure beads with self-exposure. Kilburn and Professor Shrum's perfectly respectable 1996 paper called "Ritual Disrobement at Mardi Gras: Ceremonial Exchange and Moral Order" was published by the prestigious journal *Social Forces.* Yet Kilburn said that, as he applied for teaching positions with universities, he distanced himself from the topic, which some perceived to be sexist, even though ritual disrobement was practiced by males as well as females.

Kilburn said that, according to French Quarter lore, a police strike during Carnival 1979 reduced inhibitions more than usual in the city's oldest section, allowing a blossoming of balcony exhibitionism. But flashing was not confined to the eternally debauched Vieux Carré. At some point it popped out along the parade routes as well. In 1988, *Times-Picayune* columnist Lynne Jenson interviewed a pair of "easy riders" stocking up on throws for the upcoming Thoth parade which rolls through the staid streets of Uptown New Orleans. As the men shopped in one of the many Accent Annex Carnival throw emporiums, they explained their selection strategies. The buddies had picked out especially long plastic necklaces, because, as rider Chuck Walston explained, "Some women expose their breasts for the long beads. That's why you buy a gross of them." The nearer to the end of the parade, Walston said, "the better it gets, because people have had more time to get intoxicated."

University of California, Berkeley, professor Laurie Wilkie's 2014 textbook *Strung Out on Archaeology* is an astonishingly detailed 421-page study of Mardi Gras bead customs, based on two decades of research, observation, and participation in the Carnival phenomenon. No one is more sharp-eyed or attentive. In the French Quarter, Wilkie points out, bead-induced exhibitionism may involve both males and females, but along the parade routes, only women seemed to flash for beads. The reason for the "gender-specific development," she deduced, is because most float riders are men and it's simply physically harder for male flashers to make themselves seen in a tightly packed parade throng. Women, she pointed out, riding on men's shoulders, could easily expose their upper torsos, while men would have more trouble making their private parts public. Wilkie's research revealed an escalating cycle of beads-for-exposure by both sexes through the 1980s and into the twenty-first century. "The material evidence demonstrates that some maskers clearly came to Carnival with the intention to solicit displays of nudity by purchasing high 'quality' pearl beads," Wilkie wrote. And "the beads most valued by parade-goers could usually only be obtained by women if they flashed their body parts."

From a feminist perspective, Wilkie wrote, the eroticized aspect of the throwing game allows men to demonstrate their ability to "buy sexual access to women through bead wealth," reinforcing their societal power. Women who collect the most prized beads may prove their "sexual desirability to others at the parade." But, Wilkie notes, from a feminist point of view they might be "dupes to the patriarchal system." Or maybe they are subversively "attempting to demonstrate their ownership of their own bodies by flouting conventions that frown upon public nudity." There are probably several simultaneous subtexts at play. In any case, some flashers face a conundrum that can rob them of the riches they desire. The "classic" lifting of the bottom of the loosely fitted T-shirt "up and over," Wilkie wrote, occupies the flasher's hands for so long that "the surrounding crowd gets a good bit of the bead wealth intended for the half-naked woman."

By 1995, wanton nudity among parade-goers had become a crisis. A story in the *Times-Picayune* on Fat Tuesday of that year reported that "Bourbon Street was a sea of skin" for two weekends before the big day. "The activity has developed in some instances into open groping," the alarming article advised. And the indecencies had spread beyond the reaches of the French Quarter into the less-routinely ribald Uptown realm. Rex spokesman William Grace Jr. declared that nudity had increased over the years "to a level that is intolerable." Grace laid the blame on college students who mistook New Orleans's pre-Lenten Bacchanalia for spring break. Things were so out of control that City Hall cracked down on the practice. Almost, anyway. On the Monday before Mardi Gras, Mayor Marc Morial attempted to cajole Carnival revelers into keeping their shirts tucked and belts buckled. "Use a little common sense," the mayor said. "We know during Mardi Gras everyone wants to get a little bit looser than they normally get, but I ask people, men and women, to draw the line." If pushed, the mayor warned "We will enforce the public nudity laws."

Despite the mayor's admonition, a New Orleans Police Department spokesman said that, in truth, the cops could only do so much to bridle the widespread guerrilla exhibitionism. "I mean, we don't have a task force or anything," the NOPD spokesman said. In other words, the police didn't intend to "shinny up balcony poles in hot pursuit," wrote *Times-Picayune* reporter Christopher Cooper, with scantly disguised amusement. The police weren't the only ones who lacked zeal. A mayor-appointed committee of krewe leaders set out to compose a new ordinance to officially express the establishment's disdain for the indecent displays, which included a growing incidence of "al fresco sex acts." But no such decree appeared. Rex spokesman Grace, who served on the committee, sheepishly announced, "We're preparing an ordinance, but we ran out of time this year."

Three years later, the city was apparently finally ready to leap into action to curb anatomical displays. With his customary, comic cynicism, longtime *Times-Picayune* columnist James Gill surmised that City Hall had finally figured out how to turn a profit on the practice, by ticketing flashers. According to Gill, during the last weekend of the last Carnival of the twentieth century "1,500 errant revelers were arrested and hauled into Municipal Court." The vast majority were male offenders, whom Gill poetically described as "unzipped vulgarians." Some had opened the barn door for beads; some merely to relieve themselves, sans available restrooms. The penalty for either behavior was as much as $300 and humiliating hours spent in the

Tulane Avenue hoosegow. In Gill's view, the cops' concentration on males smacked of unfairness. After all, he wrote, exposed breasts were much more common. If bare breasts were not exactly a dime a dozen, "it is only because of inflation in the price of beads," he added. Of the many, many arrestees, only a handful were women, meaning "there is something decidedly fishy about this year's arrest statistics," Gill concluded. "For many offenders, the time spent in jail must be a much worse punishment than the fine," Gill wrote. "Female exhibitionists must be grateful that the cops were generally too gallant to subject them to such a disagreeable experience."

As an aside, Gill's column made reference to the popular series of *Girls Gone Wild* videos that produced millions in profits and became a pop culture phenomenon by taping young women in the act of drunken disrobement, often on the streets of New Orleans. "The trade in racy Mardi Gras videos is said to be brisk and even international," Gill wrote. "What a shock it will be when some burgher hurries home to his VCR only to see his daughter get naked on Bourbon Street." *Girls Gone Wild,* which first appeared in 1997, would be remembered entirely for prurient exploitation, if it weren't for an act of corporate kindness in 2005. The destruction wrought by Hurricane Katrina and the failure of the federal levee system was among New Orleans's darkest moments, but it was *Girls Gone Wild*'s brightest. *GGW* founder and CEO Joe Francis dedicated tens of thousands of dollars in proceeds from the sale of taste-impaired Mardi Gras–themed products to the Red Cross to aid struggling storm and flood victims. "Year after year the city of New Orleans and its citizens have welcomed us with open arms, and we have looked forward to our yearly trip to the Big

Easy," said Francis, in a story on the CNN /Money website. "The utter destruction of New Orleans and many parts of the Gulf coast truly saddens us." The CNN/Money story noted that the New Orleans–shot video *Girls Gone Wild Doggystyle* with superstar rapper Snoop Dogg was one of the company's most sought-after titles.

On the subject of sexual puns, in Professor Wilkie's telling, pearl-style plastic beads have a special connotation. During the AIDS epidemic, she explained, a "pearl necklace" was code for a certain safe-sex practice, "more politely known as mammary sex," which was coyly referred to in a popular 1981 ZZ Top song titled, well, "Pearl Necklace." Wilkie believes the term was so broadly understood by throwing-game participants that it lent a mystique to large, lustrous, white beads, making them particularly popular among Carnival exhibitionists and those seeking to induce exhibitionism. Mystique can be costly. According to Stewart Yerton's 1999 *Times-Picayune* story, just before the most recent millennium, a forty-inch strand of "pearlescent white beads, about the size of ping pong balls and interspersed by smaller, shiny beads of green, gold and purple" sold for six to nine dollars in French Quarter souvenir shops, which extrapolates to roughly nine to fourteen dollars at this writing. In the bead trade, pearl beads are exceptional only because they must be made with what is known as translucent "virgin" plastic, unlike metallic beads, which can be made from recycled plastic. The use of the term "virgin plastic" vis-à-vis symbolically sexual exchanges is, of course, linguistically sublime.

6

Sex, Drugs, Rock and Roll, and the Identity Politics of Beads

"Medallion beads became all the rage in the mid '70s," wrote throw authority Jimmy Clark. Starting in the mid-1960s, he said, a few krewes might have thrown custom-made necklaces that included small medallions molded amidst the ordinary molded-on-string beads. The next step in the evolution of medallion beads was the appearance of flat, roughly three-inch, plastic disks printed with the krewe logos, hung from conventional beads by a tiny wire ring. Sometime in the 1980s, Clark laid out a then-staggering $50,000 for a specially modified machine that produced the flat medallions. The highly efficient gizmo looked like a miniature amusement-park ride, Clark said. His wife raised an eyebrow at the investment, he recalled, but it proved to be a bonanza. The machine allowed him to produce the krewes' medallion beads weeks sooner than they could be imported.

Medallion beads were the heir apparent to the doubloon, which began falling out of fashion. "The personalization of the simple bead was a transformation," Clark said. Medallions eventually evolved from thin, flat disks to elaborate bas relief sculptures, thicker than oatmeal cookies. If one medallion was good, then more were better. In time, some high-end beads were festooned with multiple medallions, like charm bracelets. The medallions were made from injection-molded plastic or cast from epoxy resin. It became commonplace for krewes to commission medallions that illustrated their annual themes. Meanwhile, entrepreneurs produced independent designs which were both marketed to float riders and sold directly to customers from French Quarter shops, thereby skipping the throwing game entirely. In the 1990s, medallion beads would become legally protected examples of intellectual property, like poems, paintings, and songs.

Sometime in the mid-1990s, businessman Alan Philipson and his son Andre had a joint epiphany. Since Mardi Gras beads often inspire the exposure of women's breasts, they reasoned, why not produce Mardi Gras beads that commemorate the practice? Why not, the Philipsons reasoned, put bare bosoms on strands of beads? With the help of a Chinese industrialist, they did just that, producing what they called "Bodacious Beads," strands of purple, green, and gold pearls augmented with a set of miniature female breasts. The world had apparently been longing for the innovation. As *Times-Picayune* reporter Pamela Coyle coyly put it in a 2000 story, "the market, well, found them titillating," and the Philipsons "boosted production to meet demand." In just two years, the inventors sold ten thousand bodacious beads at ten dollars per strand, with endless future sales in sight. The meta idea of making breasts visible on necklaces that were possibly employed to make breasts visible was only one of a pair of the Philipsons' innovations. In 1998 they patented their "Bodacious Beads," becoming the first bead designers to legally protect a product from duplication. Naturally, when breast beads by other manufacturers popped out in the marketplace, the Philipsons sued.

At trial, lawyers for the competing bead manufacturers argued that the image of nude bosoms belongs to all humankind. They disagreed that "beads shaped like female breasts, albeit in proportions that might make even Barbie blush, were eligible for patent protection," Coyle wrote. "Contending that so-called 'mammiform beads' have been around since the Bronze Age, at least 30,000 years, they offered up photographs of ancient beads found in Czechoslovakia, the Jordan River Valley and Crete." With fevered courthouse grandiosity, the lawyers opposing the Philipsons declared that "the Philipsons invented neither the female breast nor the celebration of Mardi Gras. The first was perfected by God over geologic time and the second by the Church more than a millennium distant from the present date." But US District Judge Edith Brown Clement was unpersuaded. In her view, though there might be slight variations among the bead designs, plastic breast beads were plastic breast beads were plastic breast beads, and the Philipsons' competitors had clearly violated the patent. "The ordinary purchaser is likely to see, quite simply, a three-dimensional simulation of well-endowed, bare human female breasts," the judge wrote. The Philipsons' defeated competitors were made to destroy their mammiform beads and pay the Philipsons damages.

Lee Chance is jubilant after snagging a trove of beads at the Zulu Social Aid and Pleasure Club parade on Mardi Gras morning, 2011. The cultural backstory of the Zulu Club, like so many aspects of Crescent City social history, can be traced by the symbols embedded in some beads. AP Photo/Patrick Semansky.

Not long after a breast-bead controversy was settled in the US judicial system, a marijuana-leaf Mardi Gras bead controversy cropped up. According to a 2002 *Times-Picayune* story, it took a federal jury only forty minutes to determine that Carnival bead merchant Shahram Naghi had legitimately copyrighted his design for "Mystery Leaf" beads meant to appeal to a "younger crowd." Naghi explained that he'd sketched his seven-lobed, serrated leaf design and presented it to a Hong Kong manufacturer, requesting the weed beads be rendered in metallic pink, silver, purple, gold, green, and glow-in-the-dark plastic. As with the bosom beads described above, the public rewarded Naghi with a wave of sales. And as with the "Bodacious Beads," similar products soon appeared in the bead trade, sold by importers from California to Oklahoma to Rhode Island, as well as Louisiana and Mississippi. Naghi's opponents attempted to fog the issue by arguing that plastic cannabis leaf–shaped bead ornaments were already in production in China when Naghi claimed to create the design. Naghi, they said, simply bought an off-the-shelf, ganja-motif bauble and copyrighted the creation as his own. But the jury sided with Naghi, who said that for his competition to bootleg his leafy beads was "like somebody makes the bread and somebody else eats it." In total, Naghi felt that his weed-bead rivals had unfairly eaten $76,000 of his bread.

Marijuana beads soon achieved interstate market penetration and notoriety. Just a year later, in far-away Normal, Illinois, a woman was startled to discover a "strange" young man who had blundered into her bedroom. He appeared disoriented. The police reported that he was "wearing Mardi Gras beads with artificial marijuana leaves."

Having discussed medallion designs based on sex and drugs, can rock and roll be far behind? The Rolling Elvi are a much-beloved Carnival parading organization formed in 2004, in which the members drive tiny, sputtering scooters while costumed as absurdly exaggerated Elvis Presley impersonators, complete with billowing bouffants, egregious Nixon-era jumpsuits, unrepentant gold chains, and leering aviator glasses. Their behavior could be attributed to mere musical fanaticism, but it's not quite that simple. You see, the founders of the organization didn't really dig Elvis all that much. Originally, they merely aspired to drive noisy dune buggies in Carnival parades, Shriners-style, which they thought looked like fun. But dune buggies, it turned out, were too expensive, so they settled on scooters. In order to give their nascent scooter squad some sort of raison d'être, they cast around for a readily recognizable pop figure to emulate. No one is more imminently emulatable than the King of Rock and Roll, so they adopted him as a more-or-less random example of recognizable Americana. Via Elvis, they celebrate the elemental appeal of celebrity, in a pure Warholian sense. "It [the exaggerated image of Elvis Presley] could have been a billion other things," said Dr. Ray "Hollywood" Cannata, a Presbyterian preacher and devoted Elvi. But Elvis was a perfect choice, Cannata said, "because he encompasses everything from the sublime to the grotesque."

Cannata is unapologetically obsessed with the many and varied Rolling Elvi throws, from plush Elvis voodoo dolls to Elvis dog tags. He says that each year, as the moment for the throws to arrive from Asia approaches, he becomes giddy and agitated with anticipation. He has a huge collection of the catchable Rolling Elvi memorabilia and has produced a 350-page illustrated, archival catalog, complete with provenances. As you might predict, over the years, the scooter-borne krewe has commissioned custom medallions that include winged wheels, a gaudy Elvis belt buckle, a Big Daddy Roth–style "Rat Fink" Elvis character, and other images identifiable with the King's kitschy gestalt. The enigmatic 2016 Elvi medallion beads feature a purple-winged, bespectacled owl that would seem to better befit Harry Potter than Elvis Aaron Presley. Even Reverend Cannata, the krewe's beyond-devoted volunteer archivist, has no idea what the medallion was supposed to symbolize. It doesn't much matter. If the mysterious Harry Potter medallion meant nothing else, it meant that the strand of beads that bore it was special. "Like the juiciest of e-mails" the most desirable beads come with attachments, wrote *Times-Picayune* reporter Karen Taylor Gist in 2008. "My teenage son came home with a miniature bottle of Jägermeister [fake] swinging from his neck." Plain old beads, even long strands, had become paltry by comparison, Gist pointed out. "Yes, even the 48-inchers have to have added sex appeal," she wrote.

As of August 29, 2005, Hurricane Katrina was the most powerful hurricane to have ever entered the Gulf of Mexico. On that day, it mowed across the narrow delta of the Mississippi River at the town of Buras, then roared ashore in Mississippi, roughly fifty miles from downtown New Orleans. Winds scourged the Crescent City, toppling trees, brushing away power lines like cobwebs, scalping the roofing from the Superdome, sending the shattered windows of high-rise buildings into the streets below, and otherwise causing havoc. But it wasn't the ferocious wind that ruined 75 percent of New Orleans and killed eighteen hundred residents; it was the flood that accompanied the storm. New Orleanians, most of whom had evacuated, soon learned that the presumably protective ring of federally built levees that surrounded the city had proved to be no match for the surging brown water that assaulted them. The bowl, as the low-lying area inside the levees was called, had filled to the brim. If the levees had held, Katrina would probably be a fading memory in the minds of New Orleanians, not a mental tattoo.

Less than four months after the storm and flood, when Mayor Ray

Nagin announced that Carnival 2006 would take place despite the catastrophe, much of the population was still stranded out of town where they'd fled at Katrina's approach. Returning residents were packed into tiny government-issued Federal Emergency Management Agency trailer homes, carcasses of flooded cars were commonplace, the National Guard patrolled the often-lightless streets as if the flood zone were a war zone, and a weird waterline ribboned through much of the city, like the devil's bathtub ring, marking where gravity had finally stopped the inundation. Only the so-called "sliver by the river," a stretch of high ground near the Mississippi River, and a few other regions had stayed dry. Luckily, it was the sliver in which most Mardi Gras parades rolled. But to celebrate Carnival in 2006 was an emotional conundrum for the City That Care Forgot. Some felt, with the disruption and deaths so recent, it was too soon to cut loose. Temple Sinai rabbi Edward Paul Cohn was unequivocal. "Thousands are still homeless and dispersed," he wrote in a *Times-Picayune* editorial. "The dead have not all been found or identified. Suffering is widespread and profound. Too little time has passed since Hurricanes Katrina and Rita [which occurred less than a month later] for us to celebrate Mardi Gras. I believe it ought to have been canceled."

On the other hand, a letter to the *Times-Picayune* editor from someone named DeeDee Roussel captured the catharsis of the moment. "Thank you krewes, for parading in the cold damp weather, with hand-lettered titles [the signs that caption each float], with throws bought or saved," Roussel wrote. "Thank you, marching bands, for performing in the chilling mist with borrowed instruments and half of your members absent. Thank you, police officers, for standing to protect us during this wispy, poignant, brave new Mardi Gras. Thank you for being here." Some onlookers may have been ambivalent, parades may have been a bit shorter, and crowds considerably smaller, yet Carnival 2006 was a tear-evoking triumph—ask anyone whom the fates allowed to be there. The first-ever Knights of Nemesis parade rolled heroically through the utter devastation of St. Bernard Parish just south of New Orleans, floats in the Mid-City parade were cheekily wrapped with the same blue waterproof tarp that coated innumerable New Orleans rooftops, action-movie mainstay Steven Seagal was the celebrity monarch of the Orpheus parade and, for the first time in history, actual members of the Zulu nation flew in from South Africa to lead their namesake parade on Mardi Gras morning.

Hurricane Katrina altered everything, possibly including the evolution of medallion beads. It may have been Katrina that first compelled designers to begin using medallions as a medium for commemorating historic events and proffering political opinions. Gulfport, Mississippi, was more-or-less directly in the path of Katrina and was ravaged by the wind and storm surge. So, if anyone was entitled to capitalize on the event, it was the folks at Mardi Gras Supplies in Gulfport. According to a story in the Biloxi *Sun Herald,* by the height of Carnival season 2006, the company had imported and distributed forty-eight thousand strands of custom-designed, patented beads that included a medallion depicting the swirling symbol of Katrina assailing the coastlines of Louisiana, Mississippi, and Alabama. The main medallion was augmented by two other, smaller, hurricane-shaped medallions. "We're shipping all over . . . even to Germany," said the owner of Mardi Gras Supplies. Another manufacturer produced a striking strand of Katrina-oriented medallion beads that doubled as a badge of honor. The blood-red, jagged, buzz saw–shaped hurricane medallion proclaimed, "I survived Katrina." During a passionate Martin Luther King Day speech on January 16, 2006, New Orleans mayor Ray Nagin pledged that, despite the evacuation of much of the devastated city's Black population, in the end New Orleans would remain a "chocolate city." Before the storm and flood, the city had been 68 percent Black. If that part of the population wasn't able to return and rebuild, he said, "It wouldn't be New Orleans." Nagin's comments reflected predictions by some that New Orleans's demographics and culture would be forever altered by the storm. His use of the term "chocolate city," which some felt was inappropriate, became national news. It also became grist for darkly sarcastic, racially divisive medallion beads that included the phrase, coupled with miniature moldering refrigerators and other symbols of the city's ruin.

At about the time the Gulf Coast was beginning to get to its feet again after being hit by Katrina, it was dealt another staggering blow. In 2010, the enormous Deepwater Horizon oil rig exploded, burned, and sank in the Gulf of Mexico, killing eleven workers and eventually leaking almost fifty million barrels of crude oil. As an economic catastrophe befell the Crescent City, bitterly clever medallion beads soon appeared. One was adorned with a depiction of a pelican, the symbol of Louisiana, soaked in raw petroleum. Another strand of beads included a medallion labeled the "Dead Pelican Society," plus smaller medallions depicting a boarded-up seafood restaurant, an oil-splotched beach umbrella, and a shrimp boat emblazoned with a "for sale" sign.

Mansion-studded St. Charles Avenue is the Crescent City's primary Carnival parade route. From 1884 to 2017, a traffic circle at the northern end of the great thoroughfare was decorated with a six-story fluted column surmounted by a three-times-life-size statue of Robert E. Lee, the failed commander of the Confederate Army. Lee had scant relationship with New Orleans, except that, to those who erected the monument, he represented the wistful recollection of a seditious breakaway southern empire that never came to pass. To all who beheld him thereafter, the lichen-green bronze general, with his arms resolutely crossed, also stood for the city's history of slavery, sedition, institutionalized segregation, and persistent racism. Mayor Mitch Landrieu expended considerable political capital when he proposed removing Lee from the lofty position he'd occupied for 133 years, thereby ridding the parade route and the city of its Old South stigma. Not everyone approved. Vociferous protesters popped up to prevent the metallic Confederate leader from being decommissioned. But they were brushed aside, and Lee was unceremoniously plucked from his perch. Naturally, some New Orleanians lampooned the monument controversy during Carnival time. More than one down-on-his-luck General Lee wandered amidst the Mardi Gras costumers with imitation incontinent pigeons affixed to his shoulders and hat. The topic also found its way into an ironic float design or two, and a satirical dance troupe took to the streets as choreographed Confederate statues.

But other members of the citizenry envisioned Carnival as a way to earnestly advance their die-hard devotion to Lee and all he once stood for. They did so with medallion beads. As reported in the *Times-*

Picayune, the management of the Krewe of Freret "instantly imposed a lifetime ban on a guest rider, Mimi Owens, when they discovered she had thrown beads bearing the image of Robert E. Lee and the words 'Forever Lee Circle'" during the 2019 parade. The Mystic Krewe of Nyx threatened to do the same thing, if they ever found out who threw the beads bearing medallions depicting the Confederate flag. A rider in the Carrollton parade also tossed a set of Confederate flag medallion beads that landed in the hands of a five-year-old Black child near the mayor's box at Gallier Hall. Such beads were a provocation "tailor made for losers," wrote the *Times-Picayune*'s ever-fiery columnist Jarvis DeBerry. "Only losers would purchase them as throws, and only losers would want to catch them and take them home," he wrote. "The people who toss them may feel big and powerful from their elevated position on a float, but they're in the political minority in New Orleans," DeBerry concluded.

By law, beads bearing political messages of any sort are banned. New Orleans's Code of Ordinances, Section 34-28, states quite clearly that "No Mardi Gras parade participant shall knowingly throw any doubloon, trinket or other throw which conveys or communicates any commercial, political or religious message." Krewe leaders routinely remind riders of the rules, and the vast, vast majority of them abide. But could the city's ordinance violate float riders' constitutionally guaranteed freedom of speech? In a 2018 story in the *Times-Picayune,* constitutional law authority Scott Nolan, a Tulane adjunct professor, said there was really only one way to find out. If a police officer removed a rider from a float for tossing an allegedly politicized pair of beads and the rider sued the city, claiming that the ban on politicized beads was unconstitutional, "Then a court would rule on the issue," Nolan said. "I am not aware of any widespread action by city government or police cracking down on alleged political throws in the past," he added, "but that could change." Politics is also banned in float decoration. According to the Carnival code, floats mustn't display endorsements for candidates for public office or promote "any issues to be voted on in an election." But the rule is complicated by the fact that political satire is a Carnival mainstay dating back to the nineteenth century. Parades such as Krewe d'Etat, Krewe of Muses, and Knights of Chaos are like rolling political cartoon strips, with float designs that lampoon government leadership, spotlight celebrity foibles, and otherwise ridicule contemporary society. Such subversions are protected by law. As the Carnival Code clearly states, "nothing contained in this provision shall be construed to prohibit the humorous caricature of current social events and issues." But interpreting what constitutes humorous caricature can be contentious.

Every facet of Zulu Social Aid and Pleasure Club culture is represented in its beads. Most strands are molded in the club colors of black and gold, some emblazoned with a dramatic capital Z. Some medallions bear heroic depictions of the warriors from the Zulu nation in South Africa who resisted British colonialism in the nineteenth century. Others are decorated with images of modern Zulu members in the club's stylized, black-and-white facial makeup. The popular "Zulu Baby Doll" beads include a soft-plastic infant wearing club makeup, plus several king cake babies—the plastic charms hidden in a favorite Carnival pastry—interspersed among the beads. The coconut, which was part of Zulu's original tropical pastiche, pops up in various forms, from stylized plastic disks that emphasize the "face" of a natural coconut seed to full-sized plastic coconut facsimiles. The Zulu Social Aid and Pleasure Club's use of beads as throws has a special resonance since the club's namesake, the Zulu people of South Africa, have a long tradition of using beads as symbolic and decorative adornment.

The Zulu Social Aid and Pleasure Club's royalty includes, not just a king and queen, but a cast of so-called "characters" such as the Big Shot, the Witch Doctor, the Ambassador, the Mayor, the Governor, and Mr. Big Stuff, unseen anywhere else in Carnival. Some parading organizations insist on anonymity for their faux rulers, but not so Zulu. In recent years it has become customary for Zulu's satirical dignitaries to mark their parade appearances with medallion beads bearing the images of their characters and other symbols, often labeled with their real names. When the custom began is unknown, but a perusal of eBay proves that medallion beads bearing a portrait of the perpetually cigar-chomping Zulu Big Shot, portrayed that year by Armand F. Richard, were tossed to crowds in 2003.

Attorney Elroy James said that, when designing their signature custom throws, Zulu kings often choose an animal that symbolizes his career within the club and "defines us to the public." When James was elected king in 2012, he picked an Egyptian deity known as Aker that's often depicted as a pair of conjoined sphinxes. James said the regal two-headed creature befitted him because he represented both the club's past and future. Though he was a mere thirty-eight years old when crowned king, James had already been a member for twenty years. James said he'd witnessed his first Zulu parade as a young boy and was immediately swept up in the pageantry. "I didn't know what it was, but I told my mom I wanted to be in that." At age eighteen, he boldly entered the organization's den and asked the bartender how he could join. Almost immediately he was welcomed into the fold. Looking back, he said, it was great of the older guys to "take a young guy in" who didn't have a father or uncle in the group. Being elected king was "a dream of a lifetime," he said. "It was a symbol of a job well done. I had worked hard in the organization."

James said that to catch a Zulu coconut on Fat Tuesday is to receive a labor of love that represents hours of handcrafting. To receive beads bearing the coconut symbol may not be quite as exciting, but the striking necklaces are still a memento of the "authentic Zulu" experience. When parading atop the king's float, James said, he rarely threw beads. There were assistants to perform that duty, as he ceremoniously waved to his subjects. As president, James walks in the street at the head of the procession, surrounded by throngs awaiting the Zulu parade, then the Rex parade, plus the various marching groups and trucks that follow. James said it's marvelous to consider the social evolution that's taken place since the club was produced by Black working men in a segregated city more than a century ago. "When those guys formed in 1909, they formed because of exclusion," he said. "Who would have imagined that an organization formed out of exclusion would lead the parade on Mardi Gras morning with crowds as deep as you can see. I don't think they imagined that what they created would last to today."

But, as racial equity inched forward, some began to feel that Zulu's costuming had become an anachronism. In 2019, protestors assembled outside the Zulu headquarters on Broad Street, where a club meeting was taking place. Their goal was to express disapproval of the club's symbology. Activists called on the Zulu float riders to do away with their traditional black-and-white facial paint. The protesters considered the style of makeup to be a degrading vestige of the Jim Crow past, just like the Confederate monuments that had been recently removed from the cityscape. "They know good and damn well that this blackface has its roots in minstrelsy, and they are the modern-day minstrels," said protest organizer Malcolm Suber, according a WWL television report. Challenging the appropriateness of Zulu's costuming wasn't new. The organization acknowledges that the black makeup controversy began at least fifty years ago and brought the club to the brink of dissolution before it bounced back to become one of New Orleans most beloved annual processions. "In the 1960's during the height of Black awareness, it was unpopular to be a Zulu," the Zulu website reads. "Dressing in a grass skirt and donning a black face were seen as being demeaning. Large numbers of black organizations protested against the Zulu organization, and its membership dwindled to approximately 16 men." In 1969, the club had recuperated enough to make Mardi Gras history, when the city granted the organization permission to parade on Canal Street, which had been the preserve of white parading groups. According to the Louisiana State Museum website, "This route change, not typically viewed as a civil rights victory, was significant and symbolic in that an African-American carnival organization became part of the city's official Mardi Gras festivities."

To contemporary onlookers, Zulu's brand of burlesque can be

difficult to decode. *Times-Picayune* columnist Jarvis DeBerry wrote that, in his opinion, the elemental meaning of the Zulu parade was cloudy from the start. "If you're a confused Black person from out of town who's seeing the Zulu parade for the first time," he wrote, "you will almost certainly encounter a Black person born in New Orleans who explains that the Zulu parade was originally intended to mock Uptown whites in general and Rex in particular." But in DeBerry's view, the parade's satire cuts both ways. "Who was being lampooned," he asked. Was it the "rich, white people Uptown who pretended they were royalty and aristocracy every Carnival?" Or was it "the Africans who had established a kingdom on the southern tip of that continent?" In the end, DeBerry did not call on Zulu to abandon its traditions entirely. But he was clear that the time had come for Zulu to retire its signature makeup. "Zulu is still trying to work a joke that began 110 years ago," DeBerry wrote. "If comedy is the quickest to age, it's fair to ask when did black people parading around in blackened faces stop being funny."

Zulu's symbolism began in a bleak era of race relations, but New Orleans culture observer Charles Cannon doesn't think that it falls into the same category as other institutions with outdated symbols. Cannon believes it continues to serve as social subversion. "Are the Cleveland Indians and Washington Redskins actually Native American institutions, founded, owned, and staffed, at all levels, by Native Americans," he rhetorically asked in a 2017 column in the *Lens* online news source. As a predominantly Black institution, he argued, Zulu "has expropriated racist representations and inverted them as a form of anti-racist resistance." The 2019 protest at Zulu headquarters was more-or-less coincident with revelations in the national news that both the governor and the attorney general of Virginia had costumed in blackface while they were college students. The renewed attention to the embarrassing legacy of minstrel entertainment might have been what made some New Orleanians feel the time was ripe for a change in Zulu's practices. To make the situation even more complicated, white people are welcome to ride in the Zulu. Which means there are white riders wearing black facial makeup in solidarity with a Black Carnival organization, during an era when, in any other context, doing so would be seen as irredeemably racist.

Jay H. Banks, who reigned as King Zulu in 2016, designed personalized medallion beads that featured a traditional Zulu battle shield, spear, and club, which he said were meant to recall the historic fierceness of the Zulu warriors. Instead of plastic resin, Banks's medallions were made from metal, in hopes of producing a throw that would double as a piece of keepsake jewelry. Banks said he ordered a mere three thousand of the costly necklaces, which made them especially precious. In 2018, two years after Banks reigned as King Zulu, he was elected a member of the New Orleans City Council. A quarter-century earlier, Banks served as the chief of staff of City Council president and civil rights activist Dorothy Mae Taylor. Taylor gained the continuous congratulations of part of the New Orleans populace and eternal enmity from another part for crafting a 1992 ordinance that required krewes to pledge not to discriminate before they would be issued a parade permit. Tellingly, two especially calcified organizations, Comus and Momus, never rolled again. Banks is unequivocal in his view that the Zulu tradition and the memory of minstrelsy are distinct.

"Blackface and black makeup are two totally different things," he told a WWL reporter in 2019. "Blackface is a demeaning, hateful, disgusting thing that is nothing we have ever participated in." To those who call on Zulu to mask more conventionally, he said, "We're not going to change our reality because of someone else's delusions."

Banks said that the Zulu Social Aid and Pleasure Club is "as ingrained in New Orleans as gumbo or the streetcar." The experience of riding in the parade, he said, is unparalleled. "There's nothing to describe it," he said. "As loquacious as I am, it's absolutely indescribable." And the symbolism extends beyond the parade. Banks recalled waiting to check out at a grocery store during his reign as King Zulu, when a woman in front of him recognized him and offered him her place in line. He declined, but the incident reemphasized the importance of the club to residents of the city. "Zulu is Mardi Gras," he said. "The role we play is unparalleled." But, he said, "I don't expect people who are not from New Orleans to get it." The mystique is very specific, he explained. "If you happen to go to the Vatican and get touched by the pope, you won't feel the same unless you're born and raised catholic," Banks said. The 2019 protest at Zulu headquarters did not immediately result in a change of the club's customs. During the demonstration, a brass band appeared on the street. According to the WWL television account, club members chanted, "Don't mess with Zulu, don't mess with Zulu," as the band played on.

7

Eye Contact, Bad Behavior, and Tragedy

Parade routes are like old-fashioned shooting galleries, with home-made, cardboard bullseyes, butterfly nets, laundry baskets, and the like, held aloft by crowd members to test the aim of bead-flinging float riders. Innocent children are strapped into wooden seats atop ladders, where they are rewarded for their cuteness by being pelted with plastic and shaped plush, to the joy of their parents who've spent the preceding years of their lives longing for the special attention of float riders that their imperiled offspring supply. Urban legends suggest that nuns are particularly deluged by float treasure, that grandmothers plow through crowds like linebackers for fallen beads, and that particularly unethical parade-goers borrow wheelchairs in which to sit along the parade routes, exploiting a faux disability for the bounty of beads tossed by empathetic riders. The thrill of the throwing game is undeniable, yet difficult to define.

Dr. Patrick Bordnick says it probably has something to do with a powerful motivator called "intermittent, random reinforcement." Mardi Gras floats are like slot machines, he explained. You never know if you'll catch anything thrown by the passing riders or not. And you never know what you'll catch. Going to a parade is like "a treasure hunt," he said. Bordnick is the dean of the Tulane University School of Social Work and an expert in behavioral science. Better yet, he's a Mardi Gras fanatic. Despite his living in New Orleans for only four years at this writing, he has drunk deeply of the Carnival Kool-Aid. He and his wife have a glitter room—a place in their home devoted to gluing glinting decoration to the toilet plungers that they toss to lucky attendees as riders of the good-naturedly tasteless Tucks parade. The couple has a Carnival trophy room, too, where they display the dozen coveted, hand-glittered women's shoes they've caught at the Muses parade, the glittered coconut that was presented to Dean Bordnick by the president of Zulu, the riding crop he was gifted by one of the horseback dukes in the Rex parade, and the otherwise ordinary beads that were tossed to him by television star Bryan Cranston, who played master methamphetamine-maker Walter White in the TV series *Breaking Bad* and was the celebrity guest monarch of the Orpheus parade in 2020. The respected academic is not embarrassed to tell you that he stood in the crowd on St. Charles Avenue crying,

Opposite page: Evod Newton, a French Quarter mime known as the Bead Man, was the personification of the allure of plastic necklaces. This photo was taken in 1994. Photo by Joseph Thomas McDonnell III. Gift of Joseph T. McDonnell. Courtesy of The Historic New Orleans Collection, acc. no. 1994.128.1.

"Breaking Bad, Breaking Bad, Breaking Bad," as the actor passed by. "Then," Bordnick said, "he sees me and he threw me something."

Eye contact is key, Bordnick said. Riders and crowd members crave recognition and acknowledgment. "Humans love to connect," he said. Throwing and catching beads is "like smiling at someone and having them smile back. Biologically, it feels good." Bordnick said that expressing enthusiasm for the exchange is the key to his success as a champion catcher. "I'm not the tallest and I'm not the best looking," he said, yet he's the recipient of Bryan Cranston beads. A Tulane University law student named Mac Cerceo would certainly agree. Cerceo had a front-row seat for the Choctaw parade on St. Charles Avenue in 2020, when he explained his bead-catching strategy to a *Times-Picayune | New Orleans Advocate* reporter. Cerceo sat in a folding chair near the curb, chatting with pals. His neck was ringed with a few strands of beads he'd caught during the earlier Pontchartrain parade. Generally speaking, Cerceo said, he didn't take home heaps of beads the way he once did. Instead, he passes along the bounty to other parade-goers. But, he explained, it's a good idea to display a few previous catches. "The more you wear and show," he said, the more the float riders recognize that you're "invested in Mardi Gras." In short, he said, "More beads beget more beads."

Beads are the beloved party favors of the biggest party on the planet. They can also be weaponized. According to Professor Wilkie, "Sometimes you see someone acting like a jerk—stealing beads intended for a child or being too aggressive. Then you will see a masker hurl a bunch of beads at that person—or more accurately, their head." Wilkie said she does not condone such behavior, but she allows that "those who were subjected to the bad behavior reap the joy of seeing them punished." In surveying scores and scores of vintage newspaper stories about Mardi Gras beads, instances of bad behavior pop up from time to time. In the February 8, 1937, *Item,* columnist A. Labas called on Police Superintendent George Reyer to help quell a recent plague of bead-inspired antisocialism. "A new type of Mardi Gras marauder has sprung up," Labas wrote. "Trinket thugs, [of] all colors, who follow the floats from start to finish, grabbing beads and do-dahs from the very hands of children and women. These gangs jostle, abuse and make an unholy nuisance of themselves." According to Labas, tourists attending Carnival had marveled over the impunity of the "trinket thugs" and encouraged Superintendent Reyer to take immediate action. "Get right after them tonight, my boy," he wrote to the top cop, "before too much trouble develops. A swift kick or two and a belt with a club by patrolmen along the route would do the trick."

On Ash Wednesday 1958, the *States* reported that a sixty-three-year-old fellow named O'Neil Martin had been shot dead in a clash over a string of beads during the Zulu parade that took place the morning before. According to the report, Martin's wife told police that a man named John Bonnee had "crushed a pair of beads that a friend had given her." So, she said, Martin took a pistol from the glove compartment of his car, "and the shooting followed." John Bonnee and another man named Bernard McConnell were injured and taken away to Charity Hospital and were later charged with murder along with two other suspects. The newspaper account does not explain how Mr. Martin began the episode with gun in hand but ended up being the one who was shot. Perhaps the reporting was faulty. In keeping with the regrettable custom of the time, everyone involved was described as "Negro." Historic newspaper articles are acrawl with instances of racism, sexism, homophobia, classism, and xenophobia. To expunge those references would have been comforting, but it would have robbed this history of Mardi Gras beads of some of its social context. On Mardi Gras 1964, a Mr. Louis E. Daray of Kenner was accused of trying to run over a New Orleans police officer with his automobile. Daray was accused of offering the patrolman Mardi Gras beads. When his offer was rebuffed, Daray allegedly cursed, gunned the engine of his car, and aimed the vehicle at the officer. Mr. Daray was later acquitted of attempted murder charges, according to an undetailed story in the *Times-Picayune.*

Not all bead-related criminality was blue collar. In 1989 Dominick Carlone, owner of the chain of Accent Annex Carnival supply stores, pled guilty to federal tax fraud. He had been accused of soliciting phony invoices that underestimated the actual value of the beads he was buying from a Hong Kong supplier by $100,000. Carlone was sentenced to "serve six months in a halfway house and pay $75,000 in restitution to the U.S. Customs Service." By 2005, Accent Annex had fallen into debt to the tune of $1 million and filed for bankruptcy. As reported in the *Times-Picayune,* Carlone's attorney blamed an unnamed employee who had allegedly embezzled the otherwise prosperous company into oblivion. "Accent Annex is totally dead," the attorney declared, though Carlone apparently immediately began operating a company called Mardi Gras Madness from the same corporate address.

In addition to instances of uncivilized behavior, the public record includes a few instances of accidental bead-related injuries and deaths. A warning appeared in the February 26, 1954, *States:* "Be careful tonight," it read, "so that you can see the rest of the parades. Don't throw yourself under the wheels of a float for a handful of glass beads. Let's not have any fatalities this Mardi Gras season." Good advice, but in the tumult of a passing parade, it has sometimes been forgotten. At especially busy sections of the routes of Carnival parades, the crowds are kept from encroaching on the rumbling floats by stout galvanized steel barricades. But on those portions of parade paths that are left open, celebrants often swarm the enormous, unwieldy floats, vying for beads and baubles. Parade-goers carrying other parade-goers on their shoulders lurch toward the riders as if they were storming a castle wall. Kids trot along the skirts of the weighty vehicles. Some of us stoop for fallen treasure amid the jostling crowd. It's nothing short of a miracle that parade-goers almost never fall beneath the wheels of floats. But during Carnival 2020, two tragedies made the ever-present possibility of accidents abundantly clear.

"We initially took offense when the cop ordered us away from the float," wrote *Times-Picayune | Advocate* music critic Keith Spera, in an account of a death that took place during one of New Orleans's largest parades during Carnival 2020. "In time-honored Mardi Gras tradition, we'd sidled up close to Float 21 in the Krewe of Nyx parade Wednesday night as it slowed down on Magazine Street," Spera wrote. "My youngest daughter Celia was perched on my shoulders, eye-level with the lower-deck riders. Eric, a friend, held my son Sam nearby." Chillingly, Spera soon realized that he and his children were in the midst of a tragedy. "There'd been an accident," Spera wrote, "a 58-year-old woman had been killed, run over by the second section of Float 21." What had been a scene of carefree Carnival chaos had become "horrific," Spera wrote. "Emergency crews responded quickly to shield the body from view. Blood soaked the bottom of the white screen they erected." Why Geraldine Carmouche attempted to cross between the towering sections of a paused two-part float—tantamount to passing between freight cars on a railroad track—will forever be unknown.

Three days later, Joseph Sampson, another fifty-eight-year-old Carnival fan was crushed by another tandem float during the Krewe of Endymion parade on Canal Street. "One witness said the man jumped as he tried to catch a light-up throw, then landed on more beads and slipped under the float," wrote a *Times-Picayune | Advocate* reporter. "The witness said a friend of the man tried in vain to drag him out from under the float. Meanwhile, others tried desperately to get the attention of float riders and the driver to get the float to stop, but it was difficult to do so over the din." Sampson's daughter-in-law Latasha Green said that there were rumors that he'd been pushed from behind by other members of the enthusiastic crowd, but she refused to cast blame. "It is something we all know can happen either way [at] Mardi Gras when adults are running up for beads," Green said. "We don't feel it was done on purpose. It was just . . . an unfortunate incident."

A poignant impromptu shrine that popped up near the site of the first accident included flowers, candles, and, of course, strands of beads. Glittering beads are occasionally seen in New Orleans cem-

eteries, left behind like bouquets. Asked to name the strangest medallion beads he was ever commissioned to create, bead mogul Dan
Kelly recalled a strand adorned with tennis rackets and Louisiana
State University symbols to be dispensed at the funeral of someone's
formerly fun-loving, deceased uncle.

It doesn't have to be Carnival time for beads to play a role in
Crescent City culture. They are always a part of New Orleans–centric
advertising, the celebrations of visiting conventioneers, and souvenir
sales. At times, they have been ingredients in street performances,
superstitious rituals, craft, and high art. In roughly 1990, a sparkling
personage appeared on the flagstones around Jackson Square. From
the crown of his head to the tops of his well-worn shoes, he was
coated in a cascade of Mardi Gras bead strands that swished and
clattered when he walked. And when he stood frozen in place like a
statue, as he did for much of each day, he achieved a certain strange
elegance. To the eyes of tourists, Evod Newton was the essence of the
glittering excess of Carnival. He was the Bead Man. But he wasn't the
first. "The original Bead Man was a guy named Jeff, who was the bead
man for I don't know how long," Newton told *Times-Picayune* reporter
David Cuthbert during a 1996 interview. "Before he passed away from
AIDS, he sold me his bead coat and I made the wig." Newton's wig
included a curtain of bead bangs that hung straight across his forehead, and a helmet of dangling strands covering his skull and neck.
Heaven only knows what his entire costume might have weighed.
Newton distinguished himself among the French Quarter mimes by
his costume, and his skill at producing what he called "bead origami,"
tiny dogs, crosses, and flowers made from twisted beads, which he

exchanged for tips. "If you're cheap, I take pennies," he was known to say. "If you're a Democrat, I take food stamps. If you're a Republican, I take cash!" The tiny "bead origami" dogs that Newton made for the amusement of tourists are also known as bead poodles. In 2012, fifty large-scale, fiberglass sculptures in the shape of bead poodles were sold and displayed across the New Orleans area to benefit the Louisiana Society for the Prevention of Cruelty to Animals.

Evod ("dove" spelled backwards) wasn't alone in turning a certain affinity for beads into a New Orleans persona. At about the same time that he was striking poses on Vieux Carré corners, there was a gaunt woman slowly stalking the sidewalks, sometimes in a shawl, sometimes wearing a motorcycle helmet. In a gruff voice and difficult-to-pinpoint accent, she asked passersby if they were interested in purchasing a "lucky" bead. Lucky beads appeared to be ordinary Mardi Gras beads snipped from their strands. But metaphysical qualities such as luck, of course, are usually invisible. Her sales pitch had a certain implied threat. A dollar or two could bring good fortune, but a rebuke would certainly lead to some witchy wrath, or at least that was the general supposition. To one and all, she was known as the Bead Lady. Self-taught artist Bob Shaffer, known for colorful painting textured with bottle caps and scrap tin, claims to have purchased and swallowed one of the Bead Lady's lucky beads many years ago in a French Quarter bar, when his career was just beginning. Or was it a lucky bean, like those tossed during the Italian American St. Joseph's Day parade in the French Quarter? Shaffer isn't 100 percent sure. Swallowing the bead or bean wasn't required, but Shaffer did so anyway. Though Shaffer does not attribute his subsequent success to that episode, he did indeed succeed thereafter, becoming one of New Orleans's most popular artists, better known as Dr. Bob.

Like so many New Orleans institutions, the Bead Lady seemed to have disappeared at about the time of Hurricane Katrina. Or had she vanished a few years before? It was hard to say. A 2011 article by Rabbi Mendel Rivkin on the COLLIVE website unveiled the poignant back-story of the mysterious Bead Lady. She was Leah Shpock-Luzovsky and, according to Rivkin, she'd served in the Israeli military in the 1950s before attending the University of California, Berkeley, on a full academic scholarship. But, the rabbi wrote, "Sometime during or after her four-year stint at Berkeley, Leah experienced a severe mental breakdown. One can only speculate that the rampant hard-core drug use in that era contributed to her situation." At that juncture Shpock-Luzovsky apparently dropped out of conventional society and found her way to New Orleans. She spent the next four decades there, residing for a time at the Hummingbird Hotel, which was known for its twenty-four-hour diner, where taxi drivers, the homeless, and the nightclub set found themselves side by side. In 2007, Rivkin wrote, Shpock-Luzovsky's brother located her in the final years of her life at the East Louisiana State Hospital, "a state psychiatric ward."

Their abundance, endless color variations, and the fact that they were cost-free when caught during parades, made Mardi Gras beads a design medium of their own, as commonplace and kitschy in New Orleans as seashells and dried starfish in Florida. With the advent of the plastic bead era, school kids, hobbyists, and self-styled home decorators began making use of the abundant "natural" resource. Flowerpots, lampshades, tabletops, bicycles, more than one automobile, and even telephone poles have been encrusted with Carnival beads. If their kitchen ovens were capable of reaching 350 degrees, New Orleanians melted arrangements of Mardi Gras beads into snack trays, fruit bowls, and tacky translucent versions of Tiffany lamps. They ignored the acrid fumes that accompanied the activity. Some fine artists put the bounty of beads to use as well. In 1959, artist John Clemmer, who would go on to become a Tulane University architecture professor, composed a Mardi Gras bead mosaic for the cover of the *Times-Picayune*'s *Dixie Roto* entertainment magazine. It's possible that he was the first fine artist to be identified with beads. He would certainly not be the last.

Birmingham, England–born artist John Lawson describes himself as a "bead pigeon," a term applied to those who scavenge the ground in the aftermath of parades, searching for necklaces others found unworthy of retrieval. Nobody exploited the high art potential embodied in Mardi Gras beads better than Lawson, who created fabulous mosaics and sculptures from the overlooked trinkets. Lawson said he was inspired to begin creating bead mosaics on a splendid Sunday afternoon at the corner of Napoleon and St. Charles avenues after Carnival parades had passed. "There was a sea of beads on the ground and a sea of beads in the trees," he said. Being surrounded by shimmering colors in the sunlight reminded him of "being in a Monet painting." But Lawson's art has more in common with the Surrealists than with the Impressionists. In the late 1990s, Lawson was the artist-in-residence at the Audubon Hotel, a sleazy-chic, rave-era bohemian bastion. Lawson decorated the hotel's fifty-three-foot bar top with a Hieronymus Bosch–inspired bead mosaic called the

"Garden of Unearthly Delights" that combined fantastical creatures invented by the fifteenth-century Dutch genius with random tongue-in-cheek images such as one of the Teletubbies, a character from a popular British children's television show. Lawson's oeuvre eventually included bead-encrusted pianos, skulls, stuffed trophy fish, abstract sculptures and, as he colorfully described them, "really bizarre kind of S and M [sado-masochistic] manikins" which "got destroyed in a party at the Audubon." Some of Lawson's works that were not destroyed ended up on the walls of museums from coast to coast. The inherent cheapness, and thereby tackiness, of beads lent Lawson's work some of its ironic punch.

German-born artist Stephan Wanger used beads mostly for their sparkling visual effect, and secondarily as symbols of ecological waste. Wanger found his way from Chicago to New Orleans in the chaotic aftermath of Hurricane Katrina. In a 2013 interview on the ViaNOLAVie website, he explained the empathy he felt for the residents of the crippled city, at a time when some pundits believed that vulnerable below–sea level neighborhoods shouldn't be rebuilt. "I thought, that is the most hurtful thing you can say to someone, that your home is not worth rebuilding," Wanger said. "They would say Germany shouldn't have been rebuilt (after World War II), because it had started two world wars. It does something to you, when people say things like that about your birthplace." Wanger, who formerly worked in the advertising industry, said he knew he had to "help somehow." The newcomer pitched in with the city's recovery, restoring homes as he immersed himself in the obstinate culture that refused to be erased by the great storm and flood. As the city recovered little by little, Wanger's pastime of decorating objects with Mardi Gras beads became his passion, then his profession. In his Magazine Street studio/gallery, Wanger used a razor blade to snip strands of Mardi Gras beads into individual orbs, which he sorted by color. He and volunteers used the rainbow array of beads to produce unimaginably laborious mosaic murals. In 2017, Guinness World Records concluded that his ninety-six-by-eight-foot mural depicting a French Quarter streetscape was the biggest beaded mosaic ever made, requiring roughly five million individual orbs. Wanger's art not only had the glittering granular surface of an injection-molded Georges Seurat, it had an integral message. In the artist's view, the staggering quantity of Mardi Gras beads that were discarded each year was ecologically unconscionable. He advocated recycling rather than disposal of beads. "Seven thousand tons of plastic Mardi Gras beads go into landfills every year," Wanger told ViaNOLAVie.

8

More and Longer

When beads didn't end up in landfills, they sometimes ended up in the city's crucial drainage system. In 2018, an industrial vacuuming machine sucked more than forty-six tons of Mardi Gras beads from the catch basins along a five-block stretch of St. Charles Avenue. The bead blockage had made one of the city's major thoroughfares vulnerable to flooding during sudden spring and summer downpours. Department of Public Works director Dani Galloway was stunned by the quantity of plastic. "Once you hear a number like that, you never go back," she said, "so we have to do better." As Galloway explained, doing better would entail "temporarily stuffing the openings with 'gutter buddies,' [flexible elongated plugs] to keep so many carnival beads from going down the drain" and "increased efforts to sweep the beads to the middle of the street during cleanup, rather than to the side where they are likely to fall into and clog storm drains." Sweeping the streets of beads and other debris after a Mardi Gras parade is like a military exercise. Hyperkinetic trash-removal battalions charge into the fray almost immediately behind the last float. Six hundred men and women are necessary to combat the superkrewe of Endymion's supermess. "A street washer truck leads the charge, dousing the trashy pavement with lemony suds," wrote a *Times-Picayune* reporter in 2017. "Workers in yellow vests rake the refuse from the gutters and off the neutral grounds. Roaring front-end loaders and miniature bulldozers plow into the piles like hungry dinosaurs. Street sweeper trucks gobble up more of the leftovers. Patrols of rakers follow, capturing the scattered plastic cups and bead wrappers left behind." Sometimes strands of beads must be shorn away from the red bristles of the brushes beneath the street-sweeping machines. Strands of glistening orbs dangle from the teeth of bulldozer shovels, like iridescent drool. In the end, dump trucks spirit it all away.

On Bourbon Street, just past midnight, mounted police officers clear the crowds at the conclusion of Mardi Gras. They are followed by workers with snow shovels who begin disposing of the Sargasso Sea of beads and other reeking debris that has marinated in spilled daiquiris and horse urine. The quantity of post–Fat Tuesday detritus is a point of perverse civic pride in New Orleans. According to folk wisdom, the more trash, the more successful the big party has been. The debris haul is announced the way rural Iowans might report the corn harvest. As reported by the *Times-Picayune* on Ash Wednesday 2019, "At least 608 tons of beer cans and booze bottles, Popeyes chicken containers, broken strands of beads and other debris had been picked up since the start of Carnival season." That number was expected to more than double as crews continued inventorying the waste they'd collected. The cleanup regularly gleans more than thirteen hundred tons of refuse, the *Times-Picayune* reported.

Mardi Gras holdout Mike Turpin cavorts as a front loader collects beads and other unspeakable debris on Bourbon Street in the wee hours of Ash Wednesday 2011. AP Photo/ Patrick Semansky.

Those Mardi Gras beads that escape the post-parade sweep-up and pass through the city's storm drains without being lodged there can be carried away with rain runoff to nearby Lake Pontchartrain, where it's easy enough to find partial strands here and there amidst the debris on the shoreline. The big body of salt water north of New Orleans links to the Gulf of Mexico and the fragmented estuary of the Mississippi River, where oysters are harvested.

Which may explain why, while dining on a dozen raw oysters at a popular restaurant in 2019, art dealer Sylvia Schmidt discovered a quarter-inch purple plastic bead inside one of the mollusks. Schmidt, an avid oyster eater, said that over the years she's found naturally occurring pearls from time to time, but a Mardi Gras bead was a first. "When I spit it out, I said, 'What the heck is this?'" she recalls. Schmidt is unsure how the bead became part of her dinner. "I don't know," she said, "don't oysters open their shells and suck stuff in?"

Back to the cleanup efforts. Finding forty-six tons of Carnival beads in a stretch of storm drains along St. Charles Avenue was a telltale sign of a growing malady known as "bead fatigue" that seems to be spreading in the Crescent City in the twenty-first century. The principal symptom is a compulsion to keep one's hands at one's sides as parades pass, to avoid the need to compete for routine, unremarkable plastic necklaces. Part of the cause of bead fatigue is the sheer quantity of throws being distributed. In a 2008 column, *Times-Picayune* editor Karen Taylor Gist expressed her wonder at the uncaught, unretrieved, unwanted beads left behind after the ALLA parade had passed. "A machine like a pot-scrubber on steroids whirled and twirled and shot powerful jolts of water to each side, pushing heavy mounds of muck and debris to the curbs," Gist wrote of the cleanup squad that immediately followed the procession. "That's where I saw them," she wrote. "Hundreds of them. Beads, apparently untouched by parade-goers' hands. A few stragglers escaped down the storm drains, but most were being rounded up by a second, scooper machine being used to herd them into piles, where workers with shovels actually strained to lift the loads into trash bins." Gist didn't use the term "bead fatigue." She described the devaluation of once-sought-after plastic necklaces as "bead inflation." It was, she wrote, "a new economic threat that even the Federal Reserve can't fix." What was bead inflation in 2008 had become runaway bead inflation by 2020. "I think Mardi Gras is at a tipping point," said Dian Winingder, who had ridden in the century-old Iris parade for half of its lifespan. "I am on the last float," she told a *Times-Picayune* reporter. "By the time we come along, people have so many beads they can't hold their heads up." For Winingder, the waste was sapping some of the fun from Carnival. "In New Orleans we're always slow learners," she said, "but it's starting to dawn on us that we're not doing the right thing."

Adding to bead inflation and/or bead fatigue were technological advances that would have been unthinkable back when the arms race began. In the 2000s, medallion beads entered the fourth dimension. Many necklaces were available illuminated by light-emitting diodes, so that they glowed and blinked as they flew through the New Orleans night. Approaching floats began looking like rolling hives of fireflies, and the necks of parade-goers pulsed with luminescence as if we'd all become wizards or pixies. Nighttime parades were never so beautiful, and ordinary plastic necklaces never seems so paltry.

Bead importer Dan Kelly confirmed that, in the second decade of the twenty-first century, blinking beads are the most coveted necklaces of all. Carnival authority Arthur Hardy, whose annual Mardi Gras guide has been the go-to playbook for parade attendees for four decades, said that in 2005 an entrepreneur named Michael Hunt introduced yet another bit of gadgetry to Carnival beads. Hunts' beads not only blinked, they also played a digital tune. But the fad didn't seem to last long, Hardy said. Perhaps parade-goers felt that marching bands provided all the soundtrack necessary for passing parades. In addition to the drums of those marching bands there was another rumbling in the distance. Even before the millennium, there was a growing public concern about the wisdom, honorability, and even morality of New Orleanians tossing tons and tons and tons of imported plastic beads to ourselves each Carnival season. Creepy whispers about sweatshop labor, petrochemical pollution, and carcinogenic contamination crept into the ears of concerned Crescent City residents. If, as lore would have it, the King of Carnival commanded that the tossing of beads become an institution in 1921, by 2021, the bead era might have begun inching toward its twilight.

Roland Barthes, French cultural observer, wrote that the operators of plastic molding machines are "half god and half robot." Videographer David Redmon discovered that they were neither. One of the wakeup calls of New Orleans's bead addiction was Redmon's devilishly deadpan 2005 documentary titled *Mardi Gras: Made in China* that contrasts the randy frivolity of Carnival in New Orleans with what seems to be the stultifying toil of the mostly female workers in a massive Mardi Gras bead factory in Fuzhou, China. Redmon's cameras capture these rural Chinese teenagers using grimy, smoldering machinery and elbow grease to mold, color, and package throws for our beloved parades. Their hours are unconscionably long and the pay unbelievably low—the hourly wage is said to be ten cents. The severe-looking compound where they live and work for six days each week is disconcertedly surrounded by walls and barbed wire, and the Dickensian factory owner seems proud of the discipline doled out in the form of docked pay to keep his employees in line. Daily quotas are necessary, he leers; "otherwise they will go to the toilet too much." The bead-making workforce is predominantly female because, the factory owner explains, it's "easier for us to control lady workers." Redmon points out that a version of free-market economy popped up in Red China in 1978, two years after the death of Chairman Mao, at about the same time that breasts and penises began regularly popping out in exchange for plastic beads in the French Quarter. When shown a snapshot of an American disrobing for beads, one of the young factory workers exclaimed, "How is that possible? We Chinese are different than Americans in that respect. We are not used to things like that," she said. "They are crazy." Elsewhere in the film, Redmon shares footage of the factory workers sanding medallions shaped like nude female torsos that would soon bob at the bottom of a strand of beads.

Mardi Gras: Made in China is like a dissection. It's meant to expose the icky innards of globalization that we might have suspected were there but would rather not have to behold. In the documentary, a young man vacationing in the Crescent City sums up our collective craving for ignorance perfectly. When he's informed of the plight of the Chinese laborers, he cries: "Get away, get away, don't bring my conscience into this." When Redmon asks bead importer Dom Carlone—yes the same Dom Carlone who was convicted of swindling the IRS, while simultaneously being swindled by and employee—how he could be a party to a business that allows such income inequity, Carlone answers: "If I didn't do it, somebody else was going to do it." Not everyone shared Redmon's dour view of the People's Republic of China's mode of bead manufacturing. When founders of the feminist Krewe of Muses visited the Chinese source of their mass-produced throws in 2005, they were relieved at the conditions they encountered. In 2012, Muses charter member Virginia Saussy told Alex Rawls, the editor of *Offbeat* magazine, that she had been "kind of freaked out" when she'd seen "a horrifying documentary on bead factories." The documentary was presumably Redmon's. But, Saussy said, "the bead factory was really nice, actually. It had a purple, green, and gold entrance and everyone wore purple, green, and gold uniforms." Muses captain Staci Rosenberg said that she and Saussy's long-ago visit to the factory near Guangzhou was very brief, but she agreed that "there was nothing that would jump out and say 'This is horrible.'" Saussy said that the factory owner asked her not to describe the ignoble fate of the beads to the young women who produced them, because "they think they're making very popular jewelry." Saussy told Rawls that, in fact, the young women were correct. The jewelry they made was "Extremely popular and in demand for a very brief period." Carnival authority Arthur Hardy also visited a Chinese bead factory and was also asked to avoid discussing the undignified final disposition of most necklaces. Hardy said he observed a line of young men carrying heavy bags of unmelted plastic pellets or some such material. He asked the factory owner why there wasn't some more efficient, mechanical manor of conveying the raw material. The industrialist explained that to install such a labor-saving device would cost the line of young men their jobs.

If Redmon's video of sweatshop-ish labor practices in faraway Asia weren't enough to complicate parade-goers' view of the throw-and-catch custom, there was also the suggestion that the glittering imported beads contained unhealthy levels of lead that could end up in the bloodstreams of Crescent City children. Dr. Holly Groh, a New Orleans eye surgeon, mother, and public health advocate, became disenchanted with plastic beads during the Deepwater Horizon disaster in 2010. Ecological passions ran high as the seemingly uncappable sunken rig dumped unprecedented amounts of crude oil into the Gulf of Mexico. Groh came to view the annual blizzard of petroleum-based beads as the same sort of pollution crisis as the mega–oil leak. So, she founded a bead-awareness organization called Verdi Gras with the slogan "Mardi Gras is about the show, not the throw," and began advocating for post-parade recycling. In addition to their deleterious ecological implications, the doctor suspected that the sparkling beads themselves could be unhealthy for children. When she sent samples to laboratories, her fears seemed to be confirmed. According to a 2013 story in the *Times-Picayune,* a researcher at the Ecology Center in Ann Arbor, Michigan, determined that over 60 percent of the 143 strands of beads and other throws tested had concentrations of lead over limits allowed in children's products. One especially egregious green necklace had three hundred times the limit. But the lead content was a moot point, Groh discovered. Since the beads were intended to be hung around the neck, the lead content wasn't an immediate threat to most people, and therefore their importation and distribution weren't prohibited in Louisiana. The problem, Groh said, could arise when children gum the strands—which every teething kid in the plastic-bead era has doubtlessly done.

And lead wasn't the only component in beads that the Michigander watchdogs found disagreeable. The Ecology Center post titled "Holiday and Mardi Gras Bead Report" includes tiny mugshots of each type of bead tested—Hermes, Muse, and Thoth beads appear in the lineup—beside lists of their alleged offenses, including arsenic content, cadmium content, mercury content, and so on. In a 2020 update, the toxicity watchdogs announced that flame retardants that might be traced to pulverized parts of electronic devices that were blended into the recycled plastic used to produce beads turned up in the majority of the samples they tested. "A number of flame retardants are known endocrine disruptors and some are linked to cancer," they chilling reported. "If you have Mardi Gras beads, do not allow children or adults to put them in their mouths and always wash hands after handling the beads," the Ecology Center advises. "Also consider bringing baby wipes to the parade to wipe children's hands after catching and playing with beads and before eating. Wash the beads that have been caught, especially if they were lying on the ground."

The health conscious, the ecologically minded, those promoting local industry over foreign manufacturing, even bead importers attempting to stay ahead of popular trends, have all taken steps to mitigate the glut of beads. In a low-slung, nondescript building, in a low-slung nondescript industrial area just outside of New Orleans, lies Arc of Greater New Orleans, a place where Mardi Gras beads go to be reborn. There, among enormous cardboard cartons of previously thrown beads and baubles, workers untangle, sort, and repackage donated beads for reuse. Those seeking crawfish sacks stuffed with recycled Krewe d'Etat, Nyx, Bacchus, or any other branded beads find their way to ArcGNO. In need of several dozen strands of seventy-two-inch silver beads? ArcGNO can probably fix you up. A rainbow assortment of medium strands? ArcGNO has them, by the ton. In the ArcGNO showroom, ecologically inclined or altruistic or bargain-seeking parade-riders gather resurrected parade booty in wheelbarrows. "It's very clear from where we stand that a critical mass of interest and excitement about recycling and being a little greener has happened over the past 12 months," said Stephen Sauer, the director the nonprofit organization, in a 2020 interview with a *Times-Picayune | New Orleans Advocate* reporter. "Three years ago, we took in about 20 tons," Sauer said. "Two years ago, 60 tons. The past year's intake was 186.5 tons."

In 2012, ArcGNO debuted a so-called "Catch and Release" trailer, decorated with a clown-face target. The conveyance was designed to reverse the bead-catching process. The trailer, marked with a bull's-eye, which was towed at the tail of parades, was a target where parade-goers could unburden themselves of the bounty they'd recently caught. In its first outing with the Little Rascals kid's parade in suburban New Orleans, the trailer was pelted with a thousand pounds of recyclables. Most of ArcGNO's annual stock is donated more conventionally, by parade-goers who can't bring themselves to see their once-precious catchlings trundled away by a trash truck. ArcGNO's purpose isn't just reselling throws. It's mission is, as the ArcGNO's website puts it, to provide New Orleanians with intellectual disabilities "opportunities to develop, function, and live to their fullest potential." It is they, aided by volunteers, who are behind the ever-expanding secondary bead market. In 2020, the leadership of the suburban Krewe of Centurions purchased all 775 sacks of beads that were sold to its members from ArcGNO. The most noble of ArcGNO's customers is Rex, whose quartermaster Steven Ellis vowed "will buy any Rex items you can give us, as fast as you can collect them."

Bead mogul Dan Kelly said that, despite the buzz about bead fatigue, imported bead sales aren't down. But bead buyers are increasingly more discerning. Instead of large quantities of dismissible beads, riders are stocking up on fewer, higher quality, more desirable necklaces. In the future, Kelly said, he won't be surprised if ecologically concerned float riders will be able to have their cake and eat it too. "I know that there are a lot of people trying to come up with the biggest, best, eco-friendly material" from which to make biodegradable beads, Kelly mused. "You can only imagine with the technology that is evolving; you'll see a whole new world," he said. Marcus Ciko lumbered along in the Joan of Arc parade 2019 wearing a hundred-pound suit of armor. The armor was not something you would have seen back in the Hundred Years' War when the Maid of Orleans became a hero, nor was it made of sword-deflecting iron. Ciko's suit was modeled after Dragon Ball Z Saiyan battle armor, and it was made from one-quarter million carefully twisted Mardi Gras bead necklaces. Ciko has made three similar suits since the start of the twentieth century, as well as innumerable twisted-bead necklace designs that look like the Carnival equivalent of fractals. And that's not all he's been up to. As reported in a 2019 *Times-Picayune* story, Ciko is questing after the dream of a biodegradable plastic substitute to produce beads that might melt into the earth instead of languishing for decades in a landfill. So far, Ciko's goal has apparently remained just out of reach.

According to a 2019 article on the *Smithsonian Magazine* website, Louisiana State University molecular biologist Naohiro Kato seems to be on the cusp of perfecting a formula for making Mardi Gras beads out of pond scum. The Japan-born scientist's breakthrough came about because of a happy accident. When a lab assistant forgot to return a test tube of algae to the refrigerator, the microscopic plants began to produce an unexpected by-product that someday could elicit cries of "throw me something mister." As a writer for the *Smithsonian Magazine* explained, "The next morning, Kato opened the lab to find a large glob of algae gathering oils on the bottom of the centrifuge. This, he saw almost immediately, could form a key ingredient for globular bioplastic beads." The upside is that Kato's beads will break down to from whence they came in more-or-less two years. The downside is that they'll be costly, about ten times the price of their imported plastic counterparts. And as of that writing, they were the color of stewed okra.

Like bald eagles, football helmets, and hamburgers, Mardi Gras beads have become unmistakable symbols of Americanness. Asked for a concluding thought about the significance of Mardi Gras beads, archeologist Laurie Wilkie referred to a phenomenon she calls "bead bleed," which means, essentially, that Mardi Gras beads aren't just for Mardi Gras anymore. Corporations, casinos, pro sports franchises, parades unrelated to Carnival, and colleges across the nation have incorporated plastic beads into their symbology. For instance, Wilkie said, students at the University of California at Berkeley can purchase molded-on-string beads in the school colors. "At a Cal football game, wearing strands of blue and gold football-shaped beads conveys the same information as painting one's face blue and yellow would," she wrote. The necklaces sold online are marketed as "rally beads," not Mardi Gras beads, but they certainly echo what Wilkie calls the throwing game, thereby demonstrating the cultural reach of Crescent City Carnival that the professor describes as "a chaotic celebration of the good, the bad and ugly of being American." It's no wonder colleges are a vector of the bead bleed. Any undergrad who has traveled to New Orleans to witness the chaotic celebration firsthand cherishes the memory and relics of the otherworldly good, bad, and ugly experience like a member of a collegiate Carnival cargo cult, proselytizing and pining for a return visit.

Carnival-style parades aren't exclusive to New Orleans. They take place in Mobile, Baton Rouge, St. Louis, Disney World, and elsewhere. It's possible that the term "throw me something mister" will eventually enter the collective lexicon of the country and maybe far beyond. Berkeley isn't the farthest outpost of the cultural hemorrhage. In 2012, as the high-tech dune buggy known as the Mars Curiosity Rover crept across the surface of the red planet, its electronic eyes lit on a strand of extraterrestrial orbs that looked very much like Mardi Gras beads. Very much. At least that's what a phony NASA press release, found on a phony—though reasonably authentic looking—NASA website, led visitors to believe. The prank was the work of Domitron Graves, a New Orleans artist and founding member of the Intergalactic Krewe of Chewbacchus, a Carnival marching group devoted to the faux mythology of *Star Wars*. As the NBC News science desk reported, despite the obvious ridiculousness of the fake announcement, the rocket scientists and, more importantly, the lawyers at the National Aeronautics and Space Administration, weren't amused. In no time, Graves told MSNBC's Alan Boyle, "he received a phone call from someone claiming to be from JPL [the Jet Propulsion Laboratory], informing him that his use of the space agency's logos was a federal offense," NBC reported. Graves agreed to pull the plug on the prank, explaining, "I'm trying not to go to jail."

In the streets of the French Quarter on Mardi Gras morning 2020, some celebrants appeared in hazmat suits. Others were costumed as Corona beer bottles and as ninja virus warriors. Ironically, as New Orleanians satirized the then-new COVID-19 virus, they were also transmitting it. That year's Carnival came to be known as a super-spreader event that plunged the city into a medical crisis. In April 2020, Mayor LaToya Cantrell announced that she was considering the possibility of cancelling the city's thirty-four parades in February 2021 to avoid a repeat of the catastrophe. Most krewes optimistically continued planning for parades by decorating floats and importing throws. Tellingly, some parading groups prudently omitted the date from their medallion beads and other items, thereby making it possible to use the throws whenever Carnival was possible again. To absolutely no one's surprise, on November 2020, City Hall announced that parades would not be permitted in 2021, owing to the continued need for social distancing. Carnival 2021 was the first cancellation since a police strike made parading impossible within the city limits in 1979. It was only the thirteenth time in history that New Orleans had officially called off mass celebrations.

Searching for a way to observe Carnival customs without violating social distancing protocols, a young woman named Megan Boudreaux advocated that Mardi Gras–starved citizens decorate their houses as if they were parade floats. Boudreaux's Krewe of House Floats became a sensation, with hundreds of elaborately decorated porches and balconies blossoming across the cityscape. The house-float phenomenon may not have been a substitute for the spectacle of passing parades, but it saved Carnival 2021 from oblivion. Naturally, on Fat Tuesday many house-float "riders" tossed beads to passersby. It wouldn't have been Mardi Gras without them.

acknowledgments

In late 2019, I was seated in a French provincial–style chair in the Rex den next to Dr. Stephen Hales, as the former King of Carnival discussed the advent of the Mardi Gras bead. Reaching into his pocket, Hales produced an example of treasure, a vintage strand of beads that he believed dated to the 1950s. They were bean-sized translucent glass gems in various colors, from pearl-white to caramel-brown to scarlet. Here and there were tiny, amber-colored, cast-glass bunches of grapes. The long-ago manufacturer had attached a strip of paper to the strand to signify its origin: Czechoslovakia.

They were amazingly elegant by twenty-first-century standards. Precious. And, as it turned out, fragile. As I handled the strand, the decades-old cotton string that bound the beads together snapped, and they fell and scattered on the purple carpet. Your author was, naturally, a touch chagrined. But Hales was reassuring. "The gods of Mardi Gras will forgive you," he said.

I would like to thank the gods of Mardi Gras, as well as the gracious Dr. Stephen Hales; unparalleled Mardi Gras bead authority Laurie A.

Wilkie; tireless Carnival chronicler Arthur Hardy; historian and archi-tect Robert J. Cangelosi Jr.; former Zulu king and current New Orleans city councilman Jay H. Banks; krewe leaders Bobby Hjortsberg, Elroy James, and Staci Rosenberg; bead businessmen Dan Kelly and Jimmy Clark; Louisiana State Museum curator Wayne Phillips; Professor Pat-rick Bordnick; Rolling Elvi archivist Ray "Hollywood" Cannata; and artists "Dr. Bob" Shaffer and John Lawson. Thanks to Marsha Bol, director emeritus of the Museum of International Folk Art in Santa Fe, who masterfully curated a 2018 exhibit titled "Beadwork Adorns the World," which was an inspiration, and who first steered me to-ward Bohemia. Thanks to Professor Wesley Shrum, Professor John C. Kilburn, and memoirist Ann Lyneah Curtis for uncovering the history of flashing for beads. Thanks to the Historic New Orleans Collection staff for helping select and acquire vintage photos. Thanks to LSU Press's acquisitions editor Jenny Keegan, who invited me to write this, my first book, and who has patiently shepherded me through the process. Thanks to music writer and old friend Alex Rawls, author and columnist Charles Cannon, and educator Melanie Tennyson for agreeing to read, comment on, and make corrections to the abun-dantly errant early versions of this text. Thanks to freelance editor Stan Ivester, for shooing away my lingering errors. Special thanks to my wife of three decades, the aforementioned Melanie Tennyson, daughter Lucille, and son Fisher, whose loving optimism and encour-agement underlie all that I accomplish. Thanks to the New Orleans Public Library and the Jefferson Parish Library. The ability to search through online archives was crucial during the height of the corona-virus pandemic when this book was written. And thanks to all the past and present newspaper writers from Pie Dufour to Stewart Yerton to Karen Taylor Gist to Jarvis DeBerry, who, as they say, penned the first draft. How on earth will history be remembered without libraries and newspapers, should they ever disappear?

notes

Introduction

2   "throwing game": Laurie A. Wilkie, *Strung Out on Archaeology* (New York: Routledge, 2016), 70.

3   a *New Orleans Times-Picayune* culture columnist: Charles L. "Pie" Dufour, "Carnival Expansion over the Years Traced," *Times-Picayune*, Feb. 13, 1966, sec. 2, p. 4.

1. It's Carnival Time

5   "I had two cannister shots": Pierre LeMoyne d'Iberville, *Iberville's Gulf Journals*, trans. and ed. Richenbourg Gaillard McWilliams (Tuscaloosa: University of Alabama Press, 1981), 53.

8   "half the population": Henri Schindler, *Mardi Gras: New Orleans* (Paris: Flammarion, 1997), 22.

8   "tossed bonbons and flowers": Schindler, *Mardi Gras,* 159.

8   "there was also a very 'floury' genius": "Mardi Gras," *Times-Picayune* (published as *Daily Picayune*), Feb. 13, 1839, 2.

8   "the appearance of a snowstorm": Charles L. "Pie" Dufour, "Ingredients Set Our Parades Apart," *Times-Picayune,* Jan. 30, 1966, 31.

8   "apparently determined to assert their right": "Mardi Gras," *Daily Picayune,* Feb. 25, 1852, 2.

8   "No Mardi Gras parade participant": "Chapter 34—Carnival, Mardi Gras," New Orleans, Louisiana—Code of Ordinances, Section 34-28, last modified Oct. 19, 2020, library.municode.com/la/new_orleans/codes/code_of_ordinances?nodeId=PTIICO_CH34CAMAGR.

9   "Boys with bags of flour": "Mardi Gras," *New Orleans Bee,* Mar. 1, 1854, 1.

10 Comus ceased rolling: Susan Finch, "22 Krewes Set to Roll," *Times-Picayune,* Jan. 17, 1992, 1.

11 "Very liberally did he along the route": "Twelfth Night Revelers: Mother Goose's Tea Party Brilliant Scene Upon the Streets," *Times-Picayune,* Jan. 7, 1871, 1 and 9.

12 "Proclamations inviting all": Stephen W. Hales, *Rex: An Illustrated History of the School of Design* (Mandeville, LA: Arthur Hardy Enterprises), 2010, 22.

12 "more than 60,000 persons": Fred E. Hamlin, "When I Was Rex, First King of the Carnival," *Times-Picayune,* Dec. 11, 1921, 81.

13 "Little has been written": Errol Laborde, "Revisiting Rex's Birthplace and Early Leaders," myNewOrleans.com, Jan. 7, 2015, www.myneworleans.com/revisiting -rexs-birthplace-and-early-leaders/.

13 "11 boxes of glass beads from Venice": Jules Leblanc ad, *The Bee,* Jan. 14, 1834, 1.

14 "There were greetings": "Mayor Flower, The Host of Guests," *Times-Picayune,* Mar. 3, 1897, 12.

15 "With Flower's election": Richard Gambino, *Vendetta: The True Story of the Largest Lynching in U.S. History* (Montreal: Guernica Editions), 2000, 130.

15 "while the show was passing": "Monarch of Merriment Makes His Twenty-Fifth Mardi Gras a Day of Delight," *Times-Picayune,* Feb. 23, 1898, 1–8.

15 "as high a figure as 50,000": "Carnival Crowd May Pass 40,000," *New Orleans Item,* Feb. 8, 1912, 1.

15–16 "Through several miles of streets": "What Mardi Gras Is: Season Really Opens January 6," *New Orleans Item,* Feb. 8, 1912, 1–6.

17 the 1913 photograph by Herbert J. Harvey: Herbert J. Harvey, Rex Parade Carnival 1913, silver gelatin print, Library of Congress Prints and Photographs Division, www .loc.gov/resource/pan.6a27381/.

2. The Arms Race

19 "resulted in the abandonment": "Mardi Gras Day, for the Sixth Time, to Go By without Celebration," *New Orleans Item,* Jan. 27, 1918, 5.

19 "soldiers and sailors dying daily": "No Masking on Mardi Gras," *Daily States,* Feb. 8, 1918, 6.

20 an enormous stockpile of explosives: Gilbert King, "Sabotage in New York Harbor," *Smithsonian Magazine,* Nov. 1, 2011, www.smithsonianmag.com/history/sabotage -in-new-york-harbor-123968672/.

20 almost one in one hundred: John Magill, "100 years ago, the Spanish flu pandemic tore through New Orleans in three terrifying weeks," Historic New Orleans Collection, Mar. 27, 2020, www.hnoc.org/publications/first-draft/100-years -ago-spanish-flu-pandemic-tore-through-new-orleans-three.

20 "a celebration such as New Orleans": "Orleans Celebration of Victory by Allies Greatest in History: Elks Stage Monster Festival," *Times-Picayune*, Nov. 12, 1918, 1.

20 "celebrating the war's end": "Orleans May Have Carnival Next Year," *New Orleans States*, Nov. 11, 1918, 1.

22 a cabal of businessmen: "Business Men Take Up Plans for Auto Races Here in Spring: Road Classic Would Bring Thousands to New Orleans, Belief," *New Orleans Item*, Jan. 5, 1919, 20.

22 "feel the need for a celebration": "Mayor to Sanction Impromptu Parades," *Times-Picayune*, Feb. 13, 1919, 6.

22 "Came Tuesday another Mardi Gras Day": Canal Street Throngs Endeavor to Revive Spirit of Mardi Gras That Made Brilliant Days Bygone," *New Orleans Item*, Mar. 4, 1919, 1 and 6.

23 "With the war so recently concluded": "Carnival Spirit Rampant, Despite Absence of Rex," *Times-Picayune*, Mar. 5, 1919, 1 and 9.

23 New Orleans was the "wettest" city: Samuel C. Hyde, "Prohibition," *64 Parishes*, undated, 64parishes.org/entry/prohibition.

23–24 A 1920 photo: Schindler, *Mardi Gras*, 62–63. The photo: "Gasquet, Float in Procession of Rex, Life's Pilgrimage," 1920, silver gelatin print, Tulane University Special Collections.

24 "A chill air smote their ribs": "Sidelines from Mardi Gras," *Times-Picayune*, Feb. 18, 1920, 9.

24 "the Duke of Victory": "Pershing Smiles Goodbye to City," *New Orleans States*, Feb. 18, 1920, 2.

24 "There was quite a litter": "Sidelines from Mardi Gras," *Times-Picayune*, Feb. 18, 1920, 9.

25 "The krewes of Momus and Proteus": Schindler, *Mardi Gras*, 160.

26 "wild rollicking and happy crowds": "Wild Rollicking and Happy Crowds Celebrate Mardi Gras," *Times-Picayune*, Feb. 9, 1921, 3.

26 "the first complete picturization": "Mardi Gras Ball Is Filmed," *Times-Picayune*, Feb. 27, 1921, 22.

27 Search YouTube: "Mardi Gras 1921: Rare Early Twentieth Century New Orleans Footage!" YouTube video, posted by npatou, 20th Century Time Machine, www.youtube.com/watch?v=FqJ_SZYckTg.

27 The Black parading group was initially inspired: Clarence A. Becknell, Thomas Price, Don Short, "History of Zulu Social Aid and Pleasure Club," Zulu Social Aid and Pleasure Club, www.kreweofzulu.com/history.

27 "Half a hundred ferocious black and white painted warriors": "King of Zululand Pays Annual Visit to New Orleans Subjects, Tuesday," *New Orleans Item*, Feb. 7, 1921, 5.

28   "clad in the jungle grass": "All Darktown Palpitates as Zulu King Parades Up Line with His Honey Bunch," *New Orleans Item,* Mar. 1, 1922, 19.

28   "the finest suit of tiger skin": "Zulu King, Gorgeous in Tiger Skins, Rules Regal Rampart Revels," *New Orleans Item,* Feb. 14, 1923, 9.

28   "represented a coconut grove": "Mardi Gras Memories Linger Despite Humility," *Times-Picayune,* Mar. 6, 1924.

28   "tossed an imperial cocoanut": "Jovial Zulu King Parades Past Mayor Walker, Tossing Royal Cocoanut as Token of Esteem," *Times-Picayune,* Feb. 22, 1928, 16.

28   "It's so great to have this opportunity": "1929 Zulu Parade," YouTube video, posted by the National Jazz Museum of Harlem, Nov. 19, 2020, www.youtube.com/watch?v=12Br4 yeT48Y&t=18s.

30   "Attention Float Maskers": Maison Blanche ad, *New Orleans States,* Feb. 19, 1922, 3.

30   "What a scramble": "Rex Again Joyously Rules New Orleans," *New Orleans Item,* Feb. 28, 1922, 2.

31   "The architecture of the floats": Schindler, *Mardi Gras,* 160.

32   "shouted himself hoarse": "Here and There Along the Sidelines During Parades," *Times-Picayune,* Feb. 18, 1931, 16.

33   A newsreel shot by cameraman Leroy Orr: "Mardi Gras—Outtakes," Fox Movietone News Story 9-226, Feb. 17, 1931, University of South Carolina, University Libraries, digital.tcl.sc.edu/digital/collection/MVTN/id/3784.

33   "Proteus promises": A. Labas, "Parade Watchers," *New Orleans Item,* Feb. 25, 1933, 1.

33   "If you don't get a bead": "Carnival Sun Out: Fair Weather Cheers," *New Orleans Item,* Feb. 13, 1934, 3.

34   "an inverted stomach": "McHenry Girl Thanks Orleanian for Rex Beads," *New Orleans Item,* Mar. 18, 1935, 21.

34   "one of the negroes": "Here and There Along the Sidelines During Parades," *Times-Picayune,* Feb. 18, 1931, 16.

34   a more nuanced peek at the Jim Crow gestalt: James P. Welsh, "Glimpses: Sleeps Through Parade, 'Makes His Own Money,' Aged Mammy Is Honored, She Shows Up Husband," *New Orleans States,* Feb. 22, 1931, 23.

35   "the President didn't throw": "Wiegand's Down the Spillway." *New Orleans Item,* Apr. 30, 1937, 14.

35   "a varicolored string of giant beads": W. M. Darling, "Rex Trails 'Giant Beads' in Pageant." *Times-Picayune,* Mar. 2, 1938, 10.

3. Bohemia, the Costume Jewelry Capital of the World

37   "Beads from Gablonz": Waltraud Neuwirth, "Beads from Gablonz," *Journal of the Society of Bead Researchers* 23 (2011): 5.

38 "By 1821 prices for glass beads": Peter Francis Jr., "The Czech Bead Story," *World of Beads Monograph Series* 2 (1979): 5.

38 "after the invention of a mold": Waltraud Neuwirth, "Beads from Gablonz," *Journal of the Society of Bead Researchers* 23 (2011): 36.

40 "very pretty and extremely low in price": Maison Blanche ad, *New Orleans States,* Feb. 19, 1922, 3.

40 Islamic prayer beads: Wilkie, *Strung Out on Archaeology* (New York: Routledge, 2016), 368, 88.

41 representatives of the German Nationalist party: J. W. Bruegel, *Czechoslovakia before Munich: The German Minority Problem and British Appeasement Policy* (London: Cambridge University Press, 1973), 63.

41 during a May Day rally: "Czechs Will 'Fight to Last Drop of Blood' Defending Liberty," *Times-Picayune,* May 2, 1938, 1.

42 Czech collaborators could soon find: "U.S. Must Revise Trade Treaty with Czechs If Nazis Grab Sudetenland: Roosevelt, Hull Study Situation," *New Orleans States,* Sept. 20, 1938, 15.

42 When Hitler's storm troopers: Igor Lukes, *Czechoslovakia between Stalin and Hitler* (New York: University of Oxford Press), 252.

42 "the Germans and their collaborators": "The Holocaust in Bohemia and Moravia," Holocaust Encyclopedia, United States Holocaust Memorial Museum, encyclopedia. ushmm.org/content/en/article/the-holocaust-in-bohemia-and-moravia.

43 "As soon as Hitler": "Where Do Carnival Costumes Come From? Answers Found," *New Orleans Item,* Jan. 27, 1939, 14.

43 Speaking of booze shortages: David Kindy, "The Invention That Won World War II," *Smithsonian Magazine,* June 3, 2019, www.smithsonianmag.com/innovation/invention-won-world-war-ii-180972327/.

44 the Crescent City's wartime gestalt: Stephen Ambrose, "New Orleans in the Second World War," transcription from lecture given July 12, 2017, National World War II Museum website, www.nationalww2museum.org/war/articles/new-orleans-second-world-war.

44 "New Orleans Knows How to Work": "New Orleans has cancelled its biggest show to put on an even bigger show," *Times-Picayune,* Feb. 17, 1942, 29.

45 "New Orleans Carnival king and queen": "Hail Rex! Symbol of Mardi Gras Tomorrow Will Be a War Bond," *New Orleans Item,* Mar. 8, 1943, 1.

45 there was no parade: "Bond Box Pops Lid at Mardi Gras Fete," *New Orleans Item,* Mar. 10, 1943, 1 and 7.

45 "baubles for barter campaign": "Mardi Gras Beads Head for Pacific," *New Orleans Item,* Dec. 14, 1943, 8.

46   "Now in stock for immediate delivery": "BEADS BEADS BEADS," *New Orleans States,* Feb. 28, 1946, 31.

46   "If one of the throws": "Find Deadly Mardi Gras Trinkets," *New Orleans Item,* Mar. 8, 1949, 18.

47   eventually authorities succeeded: "Poison Bead Drive," *New Orleans States,* May 9, 1949, 14.

47   "How eagerly they strained": "Hey, Mister, Throw Me Something!" *New Orleans Item,* Mar. 19, 1949, 3.

47–48   "the industry was allowed to decline": Francis, "The Czech Bead Story," 14.

48   "By 1947, nearly a thousand": R. M. Douglas, *Orderly and Humane: The Expulsion of the Germans after the Second World War* (New Haven, CT: Yale University Press, 2013), 311.

49   the bead trade would eventually: "Pity the Czech," *New Orleans States,* Feb. 21, 1950, 8.

49   she stumbled upon a small treasure trove: Wilkie, *Strung Out on Archaeology,* 178–79.

50   An advertisement in the *States:* "Attention Truck and Float Riders," *New Orleans States,* Feb. 7, 1953, 12.

51   "in 1942 a Czech couple": Peter Francis Jr., *Beads of the World* (Atglen, PA: Schiffer Books, 1999), 81.

51   "an immense shipment of glass beads": Maud O'Bryan, "Up and Down the Street: Beads from India Await Carnival Riders," *Times-Picayune,* Jan. 30, 1968, 11.

51   ten years after Czechoslovakia: Francis, "The Czech Bead Story," 82.

51   An enterprising flooring supplier: "Attention Float and Truck Riders!" *New Orleans States,* Feb. 7, 1953, 12.

51   "Sell to Commies": Mrs. Frederick James, "Sell to Commies, But Don't Buy, She Says," *New Orleans States Item,* Mar. 13, 1964, 10.

52   Pie Dufour defended: Charles L. "Pie" Dufour, "What's Wrong with Carnival Beads from Czechoslovakia?" *New Orleans States Item,* Feb. 18, 1964, 10.

53   reporter John Sweeney described: John Sweeney, "Scandal of slave labour in prison's glassworks," *Observer,* Aug. 14, 1988, 2.

53   "a rather tiny percentage": Peter Francis Jr., "Beads Made in Czech Prisons?" *Margaretologist: The Journal of the Center for Bead Research* 4, no. 1. (1991): 8.

54   "Beautiful heavy bead necklaces": "Attention Float and Truck Riders!" *New Orleans States,* Feb. 16, 1953, 19.

4. The Booming Bead Business

56   "Mrs. Crawford H. Ellis": "Mardi Gras," *New Orleans States,* Feb. 9, 1940, 17.

56   "witnesses to accident": "Witnesses," *Times-Picayune,* Feb. 26, 1949, 20.

57   "Three out of five strings of beads": "Carnival Parade Suggestions," *Times-Picayune,* Mar. 4, 1949, 12.

57   "Cut his hand while snagging": Thomas Griffin, "Grand Opening," *New Orleans Item,* Feb. 23, 1954, 9.

57   the mayor's wife, Corrine: Earl Wilson, "Accolade," *New Orleans Item,* Mar. 5, 1954, 9.

57   "Local legend suggests": Lissa Capo, "Throw Me Something Mister: The History of Carnival Throws in New Orleans," MA thesis, University of New Orleans, 2011, 25–26.

58   "Any person who is attending": "Limitation of liability for loss connected with Mardi Gras parades and festivities; fair and festival parades," Louisiana State Legislature Revised Statute 9:2796, 2011, law.justia.com/codes/louisiana/2011/rs/title9/rs9-2796/#:~:text =Civil%20code%2Dancillaries-,RS%209%3A2796%20%E2%80%94%20Limita-tion%200f%201iability%20for%2010ss%20connected%20with,festivities%3B%20 fair%20and%20festival%20parades.

60   "a magical operation par excellence": Roland Barthes, *Mythologies* (1957; New York: Hill and Wang, 2012), 193–95.

60   the Krewe of Endymion . . . is named: Keith Spera, "Endymion at 50: How Ed Muniz created Mardi Gras' biggest parade," *New Orleans Advocate* (online), Jan. 30, 2016.

64   Cimino's ad in the *Times-Picayune:* "For Carnival Throws . . . ," *Times-Picayune,* Feb. 8, 1966, 8.

66   a burgeoning crop of throw importers: Jimmy Clark, "A History of the Mardi Gras Throw Supply Houses: Flooring Company Gave Birth to a Multi-Million Dollar In-dustry," *Arthur Hardy's Mardi Gras Guide,* 2021.

67   "The U.S. Customs Service once subjected": Stewart Yerton, "The Bead Goes On," *Times-Picayune,* Feb. 14, 1999, F1.

67   A spasm of concern rippled: Doug MacCash, "'Good News' for Mardi Gras 2020: Bead costs won't go up after Chinese tariffs delayed," *Times-Picayune* (online), Aug. 15, 2019.

68   "Size matters": Karen Taylor Gist, "In the Throws of Bead-Flation," *Times-Picayune,* Feb. 2, 2008, Inside Out sec., 9.

5. Show Me Something, Mister . . . or Miss

73   several readers commented: Doug MacCash, "Texas artist, 65, says she was first to flash for beads in 1976," *Times-Picayune | New Orleans Advocate,* Dec. 6, 2020, A1.

75   "Bourbon Street is the Wall Street": Yerton, "The Bead Goes On," F1.

76   perfectly respectable 1996 paper: Wesley Shrum and John Kilburn, "Ritual Disrobe-ment at Mardi Gras: Ceremonial Exchange and Moral Order," *Social Forces* 75, no. 2 (December 1996): 423–58.

76   "easy riders": Lynne Jensen, "Parade Junkies Are Loaded Up and Ready to Ride," *Times-Picayune,* Feb. 11, 1988, 111.

77 "gender-specific development": Wilkie, *Strung Out on Archaeology,* 33.

78 "Bourbon Street was a sea of skin": Christopher Cooper, "Carnival Committee Targets Nudity," *Times-Picayune,* Feb. 28, 1995, 4.

79 "1,500 errant revelers": James Gill, "Viewing Southern Exposure," *Times-Picayune,* Mar. 1, 1998, 56.

80 "Year after year the city of New Orleans": "'Girls Gone Wild' for Katrina," CNN Money website, Sept. 20, 2005, money.cnn.com/2005/09/20/news/katrina_girls_gone_wild/.

81 "pearl necklace": Wilkie, *Strung Out on Archaeology,* 286.

81 "pearlescent white beads": Yerton, "The Bead Goes On," F1.

6. Sex, Drugs, Rock and Roll, and the Identity Politics of Beads

82 "Medallion beads became all the rage": Jimmy Clark, "A History of the Mardi Gras Throw Supply Houses: Flooring Company Gave Birth to a Multi-Million Dollar Industry," *Arthur Hardy's Mardi Gras Guide* (Mandeville, LA: Arthur Hardy Enterprises, 2021).

83 "the market, well": Pamela Coyle, "Carnival Bead Maker Wins 'Bodacious' Case," *Times-Picayune,* Apr. 3, 2000, B1.

85 "Mystery Leaf": Doug MacCash, "Bootleg Bead Battle—N.O. designer wins 'Mystery Leaf' case," *Times-Picayune,* June 27, 2002, 1.

86 in far-away Normal, Illinois: "Twin City man charged with detaining woman," *Bloomington Pantagraph,* Sept. 17, 2003.

88 "Like the juiciest of e-mails": Gist, "In the Throws of Bead-Flation."

89 "Thousands are still homeless": Rabbi Edward Paul Cohn, "Too soon to party," *Times-Picayune,* Feb. 23, 2006, 7.

89 "Thank you krewes": DeeDee Roussel, "Carnivals players not giving up," *Times-Picayune,* Feb. 21, 2006, 36.

90 the company had imported and distributed: Jean Prescott, "Katrina Comes Back as Mardi Gras Bead," Biloxi *Sun Herald,* Feb. 8, 2006, C14.

91 New Orleans mayor Ray Nagin pledged: John Pope, "Evoking King, Nagin calls N.O. 'chocolate' city—Speech addresses fear of losing black culture," *Times-Picayune,* Jan. 17, 2006, 1.

93 "instantly imposed a lifetime ban": Kevin Litten, "Nyx still trying to identify rider who threw Confederate flag beads," *Times-Picayune,* Mar 4, 2019, B4.

93 A rider in the Carrollton parade: Doug MacCash, "Child catches Confederate flag Mardi Gras beads at Sunday parade," *Times-Picayune* (online), Feb. 1, 2016, www.mardigras.com/new_orleans_parades/article_5537f7ca-3a6f-5d1b-8164-848a189c6c30.html.

93 "tailor made for losers": Jarvis DeBerry, "Robert E. Lee Mardi Gras beads are for losers: Opinion." *Times-Picayune* (online), Feb. 2, 2018.

93 "No Mardi Gras parade participant": "Chapter 34—Carnival, Mardi Gras," *New Orleans, Louisiana—Code of Ordinances,* Section 34-28—Prohibited throws (b), last modified Oct. 19, 2020, library.municode.com/la/new_orleans/codes/code_of_ordinances?nodeId=PTIICO_CH34CAMAGR.

93 really only one way to find out: Beau Evans, "Lee Circle beads: What code, krewes say about 'political' Mardi Gras throws," *Times-Picayune* (online), Feb. 7, 2018.

94 "nothing contained in this provision": "Chapter 34—Carnival, Mardi Gras," *New Orleans, Louisiana—Code of Ordinances,* Section 34-28—Prohibited throws (b).

97 "They know good and damn well": Danny Monteverde, "Zulu blackface protest quickly turns into parade and party," WWL television website, Feb. 21, 2019, www.wwltv.com/article/news/local/orleans/zulu-blackface-protest-quickly-turns-into-parade-and-party/289-849593b5-589c-4654-b8f4-17dde48f2dba.

97 "In the 1960's during the height": Clarence A. Becknell, Thomas Price, Don Short, "History of Zulu Social Aid and Pleasure Club," Zulu Social Aid and Pleasure Club website, www.kreweofzulu.com/history.

97 "This route change": "Zulu: From Tramps to Kings," Louisiana State Museum Online Exhibits, crt.state.la.us/louisiana-state-museum/online-exhibits/zulu-from-tramps-to-kings/index.

98 "If you're a confused Black person": Jarvis DeBerry, "The Zulu Club once scrubbed off the blackface; can it be convinced to do so again?" *Times-Picayune* (online), Feb. 20, 2019.

98 "Are the Cleveland Indians": C. W. Cannon, "Behind the Zulu blackface flap: liberal guilt, clueless outsiders," *Lens* website, Mar. 10, 2017, thelensnola.org/2017/03/10/behind-the-zulu-blackface-flap-liberal-guilt-clueless-outsiders/.

99 both the governor and the attorney general: John Eligon, "Yearbook Pages at Northam's Medical School Recorded Both Memories and Prejudices," *New York Times* (online), Feb. 5, 2019.

100 "Blackface and black makeup": Danny Monteverde, "Zulu blackface protest quickly turns into parade and party," *WWL* television website, Feb. 21, 2019, www.wwltv.com/article/news/local/orleans/zulu-blackface-protest-quickly-turns-into-parade-and-party/289-849593b5-589c-4654-b8f4-17dde48f2dba.

7. Eye Contact, Bad Behavior, and Tragedy

104 Cerceo had a front-row seat: Doug MacCash, "Are Too Many Beads Thrown at Mardi Gras? For Some Krewes, the Issue Is at a 'Tipping Point,'" *Times-Picayune | New Orleans Advocate,* Feb. 15, 2020, www.nola.com/entertainment_life/festivals/article_b683c352-4ddf-11ea-8fa9-3bf567a0cb11.html.

104 "Sometimes you see someone": Wilkie, *Strung Out on Archaeology,* 165.

105 "A new type of Mardi Gras marauder": A. Labas, "George Reyer," *New Orleans Item,* Feb. 8, 1937, 1.

105 a sixty-three-year-old fellow named O'Neil Martin: "Mardi Gras Clashes Leave 1 Dead, 1 Shot," *New Orleans States,* Feb. 19, 1958, 2.

106 Mr. Louis E. Daray of Kenner: "Accused Kenner Man Acquitted," *Times-Picayune,* June 20, 1964, 13.

106 Dominick Carlone, owner of the chain: Steve Cannizaro, "Exec Must Repay U.S. \$75,000 in Carnival-Bead Import Scam," *Times-Picayune,* June 7, 1989, B3.

106 Carlone's attorney blamed: Jaquetta White, "Bead business throws in towel—attorney says thievery sinks Accent Annex," *Times-Picayune,* June 14, 2005, Money sec., 1.

107 "Be careful tonight": "Warning," *New Orleans States,* Feb. 26, 1954, 8.

107 "We initially took offense": Keith Spera, "'Tragic, Surreal': At Fatal Nyx parade accident, a reporter shares the scene firsthand," *Times-Picayune | New Orleans Advocate,* Feb. 20, 2020, www.nola.com/entertainment_life/keith_spera/article_e452dd4a -540b-11ea-b90a-f34f919c48ba.html.

108 "One witness said the man jumped": Katy Reckdahl and Katelyn Umholtz, "Man hit and killed by Endymion float in 2nd 'horrific' accident during Mardi Gras," *Times-Picayune | New Orleans Advocate,* Feb. 22, 2020, www.nola.com/news/crime_police /article_4ac3dbba-55d8-11ea-bd4d-5bb3f7763ff8.html.

108 "It is something we all know": Ramon Antonio Vargas and Danny Monteverde, *Times-Picayune | New Orleans Advocate* (online), Feb. 23, 2020, www.nola.com/news/crime _police/article_3e19bc70-55f8-11ea-b81d-23576793d2fd.html.

109 "The original Bead Man": David Cuthbert, "To Bead or Not to Bead," *Times-Picayune,* Aug. 11, 1996, D2.

111 unveiled the poignant backstory of the mysterious Bead Lady: Rabbi Mendel Rivkin, "The Woman Named Leah," *COLLIVE,* Feb. 7, 2011, collive.com/the-woman-named -leah/.

112 artist John Clemmer: John Clemmer, *Times-Picayune Dixie Roto Magazine,* Feb. 8, 1969, cover.

113 "I thought, that is the most hurtful thing": Renée Peck, "Bead Artist Aims for New World Record," *NolaVie,* Jan. 3, 2013, www.vianolavie.org/2013/01/03/bead-artist -aims-for-new-world-record-63997/.

114 Guinness World Records concluded: Kristen Stephenson, "Artist and local New Orleans community take back the record for the largest bead mosaic," *Guinness World Record* website, May 30, 2017, www.guinnessworldrecords.com/news/commercial/2017/5 /artist-and-local-new-orleans-community-take-back-the-record-for-largest-bead -mosa-474289.

8. More and Longer

115   "Once you hear a number like that": Beau Evans, "46 tons of Mardi Gras beads found in clogged catch basins," *Times-Picayune,* Jan 25, 2018, https://www.nola.com/news /politics/article_37e0ff53-894c-5aed-b4c3-129852582269.html.

116   "A street washer truck leads the charge": Doug MacCash, "High-speed parade cleanup is a Mardi Gras miracle." *Mardi Gras.com | The Times-Picayune,* Feb. 25, 2017, https://www.mardigras.com/new_orleans_parades/article_ea191286-88c5 -589d-a591-82c6cc16e04f.html.

116   "At least 608 tons of beer cans": Williams, Jessica, "608 tons of trash, beads, more picked up as New Orleans cleans up from Mardi Gras." *New Orleans Advocate,* Mar 6, 2019, https://www.nola.com/news/article_ecce3a26-a00d-5333-b260-ad3c809f4b1f. html#:~:text=WhatsApp-,608%20tons%20of%20trash%2C%20beads%2C%20 more%20picked%20up%20as%20New,cleans%20up%20from%20Mardi%20Gras.

118   "A machine like a pot-scrubber on steroids": Gist, "In the Throws of Bead-Flation."

119   "I think Mardi Gras": MacCash, "Are too many beads thrown at Mardi Gras? For some krewes, the issue is at a 'tipping point,'" *Times-Picayune | New Orleans Advocate.* Feb. 15, 2020.

120   Redmon's devilishly deadpan 2005 documentary: David Redmon, "Mardi Gras: Made in China," *Carnival Esque Films,* 2008.

122   "kind of freaked out": Alex Rawls, "Krewe of Muses' Mardi Gras Throws," *Offbeat Magazine,* Feb. 1, 2012. https://www.offbeat.com/articles/krewe-of-muses-mardi-gras -throws/.

123   a researcher at the Ecology Center: Doug MacCash, "Are there unsafe levels of lead in Mardi Gras beads? One group says yes," *Times-Picayune,* Dec. 7, 2013, https://www .nola.com/entertainment_life/arts/article_84b6b4d6-04f6-5326-ad4a-f151709d5981 .html.

124   "A number of flame retardants": "Chemical Hazards in Mardi Gras Beads: 2020 Update," *Ecology Center.* Feb. 24, 2020, https://www.ecocenter.org/healthy-stuff/reports/mardi -gras-beads-2020-update.

125   "It's very clear from where we stand": MacCash, "Are too many beads thrown at Mardi Gras? For some krewes, the issue is at a 'tipping point,'" *Times-Picayune | New Orleans Advocate.* Feb. 15, 2020.

126   "You can only imagine": Doug MacCash, "Meet The Bead Man: He makes football jerseys and suits of armor from throws." *Mardi Gras.com | The Times-Picayune,* Mar 4, 2019, https://www.mardigras.com/new_orleans_parades/article_4bf4c06a-654c -535b-a3e9-4482ef6ab81f.html.

127   "The next morning, Kato opened": David Taylor, "Made From Microalgae, These Mardi Gras Beads Are Biodegradable," *Smithsonian Magazine online,* Feb. 27, 2019,

https://www.smithsonianmag.com/innovation/made-from-microalgae-these-mardi
-gras-beads-are-biodegradable-180971578/.

128   a phony NASA press release: Doug MacCash, "Krewe of Chewbacchus perpetrates Mars rover hoax, NASA not amused," *Times-Picayune* (online), Dec. 3,2021, https:// www.nola.com/entertainment_life/festivals/article_cd9c544b-008c-5747-ab7f -94408c18f377.html.

129   Mayor LaToya Cantrell announced: Jessica Williams, "LaToya Cantrell: Cancel- ing Mardi Gras 2021 is 'something we have to think about,'" *Times-Picayune | New Orleans Advocate* (online), Apr. 28, 2020, https://www.nola.com/news/coronavirus /article_41f55850-897d-11ea-8245-6fa0b4757d99.html.

129   City Hall announced that parades: Doug MacCash and Chad Calder, "No Mardi Gras sea- son parades in New Orleans in 2021; krewes react to 'hard moment,'" *Times-Picayune | New Orleans Advocate* (online), Nov. 17, 2020, https://www.nola.com/entertainment _life/mardi_gras/article_e5b0dd08-28dc-11eb-b8b2-939bf975bd79.html.

130   Searching for a way to observe: Doug MacCash, "Krewe of House Floats, a Mardi Gras 2021 parade alternative, is on a roll," *Times-Picayune | New Orleans Advocate,* Nov. 27, 2020, https://www.nola.com/entertainment_life/mardi_gras/article_9a3ab472-30d2 -11eb-956d-4782c0303e00.html.